A HANDS-ON
GUIDE TO
CREATING
MULTISENSORY
WORSHIP
EXPERIENCES
FOR YOUTH
MINISTRY

sacredspace

DAN KIMBALL & LILLY LEWIN

 ZONDERVAN®

ZONDERVAN.com/
AUTHORTRACKER
follow your favorite authors

 youth
specialties

**youth
specialties**

Sacred Space: A Hands-On Guide to Creating Multisensory Worship Experiences for Youth Ministry
Copyright 2008 by Dan Kimball and Lilly Lewin

Youth Specialties resources, 300 S. Pierce St., El Cajon, CA 92020 are published by Zondervan, 5300 Patterson Ave. SE, Grand Rapids, MI 49530.

ISBN 978-0-310-27111-6

Cover design by SharpSeven Design
Interior design by Brandi Etheredge Design

Printed in the United States of America

09 10 11 12 13 14 • 20 19 18 17 16 15 14 13 12 11 10 9 8 7 6 5 4 3 2

ACKNOWLEDGMENTS

Dan: I want to first acknowledge that although the title of this book is *Sacred Space*, the truth is that *all* spaces can be sacred. Declaring a space or place as *sacred* simply means we're dedicating it to God. So whether outdoors in the beauty of nature or inside a church building, all spaces can be sacred. There was an ugly, smelly, and often cold custodian's closet at Multnomah Bible College that probably was one of the most sacred spaces for prayer that I've ever had. So it's important to recognize that putting together some creative items on a table with a candle or two isn't what makes something "sacred." This is actually an important theological thing to say—we aren't promoting a dichotomy of what is sacred or secular or saying that the way something looks makes it "sacred" or not. Broom closets aren't that attractive.

Having noted that, I want to thank Hannah Mello for helping compile all the examples in this book from what we've been doing at Vintage Faith Church. Also Sarah Martin for helping get the photos of prayer stations together. Also the Vintage Faith Church Palette Team members who've been so incredibly wonderful and passionate about expressing worship and teaching Scripture in holistic ways: Josh Fox, Kristin Culman, Cheryl Isaacson, Eric Isaacson, Sarah Bishop, Brian Jenson, Lucas Brooks, Wendy Davis, Shannon Marie Cole, Liz Cantu, and the others who over the past couple of years have dedicated their prayers, time, and hearts to create sacred spaces.

Lilly: It really does take a village to create worship experiences and to write a book about them. Experiential worship doesn't happen in a vacuum, either; it's created in community. Even when I'm creating stuff on my own, it's really happening in community because of all the folks who've gone before me, all the people I've read and "borrowed" from over the years. So I am deeply grateful to all the creative souls who've inspired and moved me to try new things and realize my passion for experiential worship.

Thanks to Roger Foote and the people of Christ Church Glendale for giving me the opportunity to launch the Sacred Space service. And thanks to the Oasis-Sacred Space team: Sandy, Sarah, Joe and Sharon, Heather, Maggie, Richard and Lori, who put up with me, made it all happen, and lived to tell about it.

Special thanks to Jonny Baker of Grace for telling me I didn't need a worship leader…that *the people* are the worship leaders.

To Steve Foster of Holy Joes for introducing to me the concept of Sacred Space and allowing me to steal the name…thanks also for sharing your gifts of great coffee, Wifi, and time in your back garden.

To Mac and Hudson who've put up with their mom as their youth pastor and Sundays as workdays and have allowed me to talk shop over more dinners than they care to mention…thanks…you two are the best!

And finally, I couldn't do what I do without my amazing husband Rob. You are tangibly Jesus to me every day! Thank you for showing me his love and thank you for constantly encouraging me to use my gifts and be who God created me to be.

CONTENTS

Part 3: Holiday and Holy Day (and Other) Prayer Experiences from Lilly's Community

How to Use This Book

This is your primer to help you try new and ancient ways of prayer and teaching. In this book you'll find many ideas and resources, and we're excited about sharing them with you. We call them *experiential worship* and *experiential prayer*. Whatever *you* call these ideas—21st-century object lessons, Montessori Church, alt. worship—creating worship that engages all of the senses will bring new life to your community.

That's because experiential worship is created and experienced *in* community. It's true liturgy—the work of the people. It flows from the life of your group and all the gifts and imagination that your group members bring. Every member of your community will get to create and be able to lead. Once we tried this new way, both of us saw how much we were formally restricting and limiting people's participation in worship. We love how experiential worship activates everyone's involvement. It's changed how we view community, worship, and leadership. So we welcome you to discover a new youth ministry where you build a new community of *participants* rather than mere spectators.

What's in *Sacred Space*?

First, a variety of experiential worship and prayer ideas that you can create for your youth ministry. Within each idea we provide set-up instructions, give you lists of supplies you'll need to pull it off, offer biblical and thematic suggestions to add to the experience, and talk about options for presentation.

We also provide a **CD** that contains photographs of the various experiential worship and prayer ideas, as well as text you can use to create your own directional and instructional signs for them. We believe the photos will add visual guidance to the words in these pages and help keep you on the right track.

An important note about the sign text: When you open up the CD, you'll find all the sign text you need to give direction and inspiration to those who're participating in these worship and prayer experiences. Keep in mind that the sign text is *completely editable*. Which means you can cut text, add text, tweak text, enlarge text, reduce text, cut and paste—whatever you need or want the signs to be, your computer's capabilities are your only limits! Make the signs what you need them to be for your own purposes and context.

Don't Feel Limited!

Although we've presented our ideas and examples in a particular way in this book, don't feel limited by that. Feel free to mix and match ideas to your own liking. Combine them. Divide them up. Add to a supply list if the mood strikes you—or toss it completely and create your own. Pare things down depending upon the level of intimacy you're after. Make things work for your group's size and level of interest—and especially urgency of need.

We say this because we don't want to just give you fish—our hope and prayer is to *teach you* to fish, to inspire you to create your own way. We'd love it if these ideas and examples spurred you on to create completely original experiences!

Before You Begin

Please take some time to go through Part 1 of *Sacred Space* before attempting the experiential worship and prayer ideas. "The Whys and Hows of *Sacred Space*" contains important background information, theological explanations, ideas for creating your own team, instructions for getting started, and much more. Having this stuff down pat will greatly prepare you for doing experiential worship and prayer on your own.

Remember...

This book isn't just for reading; it's designed to be experienced. As you begin, think about your own context, your people, and how these ideas can be translated and applied your community. Dream big, don't be afraid, be open to the Holy Spirit, and allow creativity to flow.

SOME DEFINITIONS

This book will present some terms that may be unfamiliar. So here are some quick definitions:

Prayer Station. A place (table, pew, etc.) set aside for a prayer opportunity based on Scripture. It includes instructions/signs that direct participants to prayer, props and/or visuals, and usually an activity or a means of tangible response to what was just taught. For example, a **Prayer Station** on being the salt of the earth might include a table where participants eat salty pretzels to experience how eating something salty often causes you to want more—which helps us know more tangibly why Jesus wants us to be "the salt of the earth."

Prayer Room. A designated space with a group of **Prayer Stations**. Usually a **Prayer Room** is created around a scriptural theme or passage to which all its **Prayer Stations** relate. An experiential **Prayer Room** consists of **Prayer Stations** that use all five senses and may include a spot or space for writing out prayers (sometimes with large butcher paper on the walls that we call a "wailing wall"); an art station with supplies for drawing, painting, building, or sculpting prayers; and a **Chill Space**.

Chill Space. This space may include large floor pillows, cushions, journals, Bibles, pens, and a comfortable floor covering. The **Chill Space** provides a restful place for quite response and writing or a place to simply be with Jesus.

Prayer Experience. A worship gathering based on a series of **Prayer Stations** focused on a Bible passage or biblical theme. *The stations are the worship.* It can be structured, though that's not required. There's no need for an "order of service"; participants can use and experience the stations as they see fit. A typical **Sacred Space Prayer Experience** uses between eight and 12 Prayer Stations. *The stations are the sermon.*

Communal Art Expression. Rather than individuals going to stations on their own, this allows for the entire group to participate together, creating an art piece or mosaic. The art piece ties into the teaching.

(Note: Lilly's friend Eric asked if it *had* to be quiet in a **Prayer Room** or for a **Prayer Experience.** Her answer: "I believe quiet **is** important because of how noisy and loud the rest of our lives are. We ask our students to listen *for* God and to listen *to* God, yet too often we don't give them the opportunity to hear God because our worship is too loud.")

PART 1

The Whys and Hows
of *Sacred Space*

Chapter 1

What Is Experiential Worship—
and Why Should I Care?

Imagine a wall covered in butcher paper where your students are writing their prayers in colored markers, pouring out their hearts, their pain, and their fears. Writing prayers to God that they'd never speak out loud in a million years.

Imagine them running their fingers through a bin of sand to finally find a large pearl—and then realizing that God searches for them like that, and they're to search for God like that, too.

Imagine them walking into a room with an inflated raft in the center, and they're asked to physically stand in the boat and actually consider what they feel as Jesus calls them to follow him. What things keep them stuck in the raft? What fears do they feel as Jesus calls them? Then they each talk to Jesus about leaving their nets, their families, their lives—everything familiar to them—to become, like Peter, fishers of humanity.

Those are just a few of the multisensory ways to pray that involve us as participants as we respond to the Bible not just with our ears, but with our whole selves. This was the response Jesus was after—and the means by which he communicated the Kingdom of God.

Jesus told stories, painted word pictures, and used common objects that were familiar to people in his time (e.g., the lily, the fig tree, the bread on the table) to capture minds and hearts.

What if we did the same?

What if the Holy Spirit involved all of our senses in worship in addition to listening to words? What if worship weren't just black and white and scripted?

When designing worship we have to ask the question, "What do we want them to take home? What do we want them to remember, to actually *get* out of what we're teaching and doing?"

That's where experiential worship begins.

It empowers us to embrace Scripture and prayer in new ways.

It provides God encounters—opportunities to go deeper in our relationship with Jesus. Experiential worship helps us connect our stories with God's story.

So...What Is Experiential Worship?

Experiential worship brings all five senses into play. It's fresh and alive. It's active, not sedentary. It's engaging, not passive. It's new to each person, each day. It tells the story—the good news of the gospel—with touch, taste, scent, sight, and sound. It evokes tangible responses. It involves imagery—not just words. It involves individuals as well as the group—and everybody gets to respond, not just the leaders or the paid professionals. There's always something to see and do. It involves us in powerful prayer. It encourages us to respond to the biblical content.

Think about the instances in the Bible that describe the Creator's visual, tactile revelation—and the created's visual, tactile worship in response: Jacob pouring oil over a stone where he encountered God, Joshua and the stones of remembrance from the Jordan River...just to name a few.

Experiential worship means using all the means at our disposal to open similar doors to encounters, communion, and connection with God.

A Few Lessons Learned along the Way

1. We remember what we *do* twice as well as what we're *told*. Experiential worship opens the door to a higher degree of learning for youth who learn more experientially.

2. Experiential worship ideally allows youth who otherwise may not have a place to share and express their creative gifts (not just musical or speaking) to do so as part of a worship gathering.

3. Don't be discouraged if a prayer station or prayer experience doesn't connect. Just as with teaching messages, sometimes some youth may not connect with what you're doing at that particular meeting.

Chapter 2

Why We Need Experiential Worship and Sacred Space

We need experiential worship because our culture no longer "gets" or even knows the story of God. Most of our students can't tell you the difference between the Old and New Testaments or even the names of the four Gospels. Even our "churched" students don't always know how the Bible relates to their lives.

We have a problem in "church land," too. We've forgotten how to tell the story of God. And why is this?

In the late 1970s and in the 1980s, many churches viewed pews and stained glass (and other symbols) as boring and outdated. It didn't help that many of these people had negative church experiences in more traditional settings. So they changed the atmosphere and created more user-friendly churches. Worship spaces were designed without the traditional trappings such as altars, or even crosses. Now many church buildings resemble movie theaters with their stadium seating, cup holders, and large video screens.

But when they got rid of the symbols, they got rid of elements that helped "tell the story." In medieval times, elements such as stained glass and other artwork actually told the biblical narrative to many in the church who couldn't read. Even the ceilings in some church buildings were designed to look like upside-down boats to remind believers of the call to be fishers of people. The spires and steeples were reminders of God, pointing churchgoers to heaven.

On the flip side, today's liturgical/traditional churches still have loads of symbols and rituals. In the traditional liturgy each piece of the worship service tells a part of the story—even the congregants' physical movements enhance the story (e.g., making the sign of the cross, kneeling, reading a Bible passage in the midst of the congregation to show that it's God's Word for everyone). But the problem is that many in liturgical churches no longer know why they use these symbols and rituals. They've lost their meaning.

Experiential worship brings the living portions of both styles and traditions together. It gives symbols new life and helps emerging generations fall in love with God.

What's more, our lives are so visually driven today that we often don't even need words to describe things or get our point across. Therefore throwing out symbols (and then forgetting the meanings of these symbols) as a church has eliminated our ability to tell the story of God to an extremely symbolic, visual culture that's no less hungry for the good news and the story of God than any other generation. Our culture needs churches that learn again how to use symbols. People need churches that teach in ways that engage them, help them engage with God, and enable them to experience with all their senses how God relates to their everyday lives.

A Biblical Mandate

An important chapter in *The Emerging Church* discusses the Bible and worship.[1] Revisiting what was covered there, it's easy to see that the Bible very clearly speaks of worship using other means than simply words. Since *Sacred Space* discusses incorporating a variety of expressions of worship and prayer that involve various senses, it's good to understand that the concept of experiential worship and prayer does have biblical backing. For instance, when you look at worship in the Old Testament, you see that the temple in Jerusalem used much more than sermons to "get God across." Every sense was involved: You could smell the burning sacrifices and incense, hear the trumpets and temple choirs, see transcendent architecture of soaring pillars and expansive courtyards. Even the texture and colors of the priests' clothing communicated specific things about God and God's covenant with Israel.

In other places in the Scriptures you can read about other forms of worship and prayer that involve the senses:

Sense of Smell. We see in Revelation 8:4 how incense is used in worship. Throughout the Old Testament incense was common in worship (Exodus 25:6; Malachi 1:11). We see the Magi presenting Jesus with gifts that were multisensory (Matthew 2:11). Philippians 4:18 refers to "a fragrant offering...pleasing to God." Even the church itself is to be the "aroma of the knowledge of him...the pleasing aroma of Christ" (2 Corinthians 2:14-15).

Sense of Touch. We also know that the sense of touch was involved in all forms and practices of worship. Believers laid hands on others when they prayed (Acts 6:6), clapped their hands (Psalm 47:1), felt the water as they were baptized (Acts 8:38), and touched the bread in communion (1 Corinthians 11:23-24).

Sense of Taste. The sense of taste is acknowledged quite often in the Bible. Psalm 34:8 says, "Taste and see that the Lord is good." Psalm 119:103 reads, "How sweet are your words to my

[1]Dan Kimball, *The Emerging Church: Vintage Christianity for New Generations* (Grand Rapids, Zondervan, 2003) 127-131.

taste, sweeter than honey to my mouth!" In Revelation 10:10 John writes: "I took the little scroll from the angel's hand and ate it. It tasted as sweet as honey in my mouth, but when I had eaten it, my stomach turned sour." The taste of bread and wine are involved in communion (1 Corinthians 11:23-26).

Sense of Hearing. We all know to what a great degree music was involved in worship—every kind of sound of praise happened, whether from voices or from musical instruments (Psalm 150). Jesus sang (Matthew 26:30). The Scriptures were preached (Acts 2:14).

Sense of Sight. Throughout the Scriptures we see in great detail how visual worship has been. Whether it's the beauty of worship in the tabernacle (Exodus 25:3-7; 26:1-2) or in the temple (1 Kings 6:29-30), we see detailed descriptions of color, texture, and design.

The Scriptures also show God using object lessons, miraculous events, and supernatural displays of power to help people learn about and respond to the Almighty in worship. God didn't just "speak" using words; God spoke with a burning bush. God didn't just dictate the law; God wrote it with his own finger. God didn't just lead Israel through the desert; God led them with a pillar of fire. Jesus didn't simply heal the blind man; Jesus made mud with his saliva and smeared it over his eyelids.

God's prophets did outlandish things in order to communicate truth using more than words: Isaiah walked around town naked for three years; Ezekiel lay on his side for weeks on end, building little miniature villages out of mud; Jeremiah carried around rotten fruit. Even if people refused to obey the prophets' instructions, they certainly wouldn't forget what they had heard, seen, and smelled. When you look into the prophecies and descriptions in the book of Revelation, there are all kinds of colors, visuals, smells, and even tastes involved (10:10).

The Bible shows that involving more than words in worship and teaching is a valid and powerful thing to do. There isn't a biblical mandate for worshiping in only one way. When we're locked into only one way of worship and teaching, we're worshiping according to our opinions, not according to the Bible. In fact, the way in which we worship has changed through time. The Magi worshiped Jesus by bowing down (Matthew 2:11). The disciples worshiped Jesus by falling down and clasping his feet (Matthew 28:9) and sitting in a boat (Matthew 14:33). But even beyond the where's and how's of worship, the most important questions are, *Are we engaging with God?* and *Are our lives changing?*

One question we hear as we teach around the country is "Do you still believe in teaching the Bible with words?" Our answer is an emphatic "yes"! We hope you're picking that up by now. Teaching the Bible is critically important. Teaching with words is critically important.

UNDERSTANDING THE LIMITATIONS OF THE "SERMON"

Studies have shown that within a week, an incredibly high percentage of people can't recall what was taught in the sermon the week before. Think about it. *How much do you remember from the sermon last week? How about two weeks ago? Three weeks ago?* I've found you can ask the preachers themselves what they taught two weeks before—and even *they* have a hard time remembering. I'm not saying sermons aren't needed, or that they don't help people grow. At Vintage Faith Church, the sermons run 35 to 45 minutes long each week. Sermons are important.

But let's be realistic. In terms of listeners remembering and internalizing sermons—even a week or two weeks later—we often believe sermons have greater staying power than they actually do.

What we desire through experiential worship is to enhance the learning and enhance the remembering. It's important to also create ways for students to be in the Scriptures and learn outside of the worship service. In youth ministry, perhaps we can be teaching theology, apologetics, church history, and how to study the Bible as a normal part of what we do. Small groups are another major way we help students learn and develop the skills of personal Bible study. But our single gathering each week must be designed to have the maximum impact on students' lives. That's why we believe paying attention to how students learn in our main youth gatherings is very important.

—Dan Kimball

What we teach about God shapes our attitudes toward God. However, we need to also consider that teaching nonverbally is a valid and necessary (and biblical) way to teach as well.

We should always be asking ourselves, *Is how we preach based on the Bible, or is it our own particular preference?* For example, the Bible never says that we should give three- or four-point sermons. The Bible never says we should always end sermons with application points. What it says is to watch doctrine and preach with the wisdom and power of the Spirit, not our own wisdom and power. So there may be many valid ways to preach—and we rather should be asking ourselves, *Is our preaching accurate according to Scripture?* and *Is our preaching effective and changing lives?*

This book is designed to assist you in proclaiming the truths of Scripture and doing it in new ways to more deeply reach your students.

So please understand; we don't view experiential, multisensory worship as simply a fad. We don't see this as watering down the Scriptures. We see this as teaching the Scriptures in ways that help students learn and remember them.

Knowing How We Learn Is Crucial to Spiritual Growth and How We Teach

Did you know that research shows that only 20 percent of the world learns through their ears? Thus, if we want the other 80 percent of us (and our students) to "get" the story of God, then we need to teach the Bible in more ways than simply auditory (i.e., sermons or talks).

Of course this doesn't just mean simply adding a video or a slide show to your "up front" time. The latter visuals are fine, but they still make the members of your group the "audience," not the participants. Instead we need to involve them in the story—to touch it, taste it, discuss it, and place themselves in it. To experience it.

THE FOUR LEARNING STYLES
How are you using these in your worship gatherings or when you teach?

Tactile/Kinesthetic – you best learn by doing/touching
Visual – you best learn by seeing (words and pictures)
Auditory – you best learn by hearing (Fleming's VARK approach adds "**Writing/Reading**")

By the sixth grade we've usually developed a learning style that will generally remain constant the rest of our lives. According to Marlene LeFever, for every 10 students in an average sixth-grade class, one will find[2]:
  • 2 auditory learners
  • 4 visual learners
  • 4 tactile/kinesthetic learners

That means eight out of 10 people aren't taught in the ways they best learn—yet 90 percent of teaching in our churches is auditory! (What's also interesting is that most preachers are auditory learners—i.e., most preachers communicate and teach in a way that reflects their learning style. Which only is the best way that 20 percent of people learn!)

An old Chinese proverb says, "I hear and I forget; I see and I remember; I do and I understand." This is core motive of experiential prayer and worship—that students see, remember, do, and understand the Scriptures.

[2]Marlene LeFever, Learning Styles: *Reaching Everyone God Gave You to Teach* (David C. Cook, 2002).

Chapter 3

How We Got Started:
Our Journeys to Experiential Worship

Lilly's Journey

Once upon a time, I believed that worship was what we did for 20-plus minutes before the pastor got up and gave the sermon or talk. Worship was singing choruses, and even hymns, boldly, loudly. Belting out love songs to Jesus, lifting my hands high, and getting caught up in the moment. For a long time, that's really where I experienced God—in the music of the service, not the message.

Then I took a position as youth pastor in a 150-year-old Episcopal church. And the longer I worked with my new group of students who'd grown up with the "hits of the 1650s," the quicker I realized that worship was a great deal more than that. And as much as I loved singing, Jesus began to expand my horizons and teach me about the power of worship beyond singing and music.

When I arrived in the summer of 1998, Christ Church Glendale didn't even own an overhead projector. The senior high youth group consisted of three students, including the minister's son. These students didn't listen to Christian music and had never heard of the stuff I loved to sing. We started building a group with the middle school students, using the new overhead projector I'd purchased and singing along with a CD to open our group times together. They seemed to like the Lost and Found songs and could even get into "Lord I Lift Your Name on High," but it was usually the girls who sang and the guys who stared at the screen.

One summer I took our students to a weeklong outreach project with 600-plus middle school and high school students from around the country who were there to learn to serve their city (e.g., giving away free soda, cleaning toilets, sponsoring free car washes, etc.). I was excited that my students would get to actually do outreach, but even more that they'd experience great worship—you know, the kind with a band…great music…songs of praise…hands lifted high…

Was I ever wrong! Instead they sat in the back row while other kids around them stood for 20-plus minutes, some going down front to raise their hands. My kids counted how many times we sang the same words over and over again: "Hey Lil, we sang 'my glorious' 81 times!"

For them, this wasn't worship; this was torture. Singing for an extended period of time when you don't know the songs, and it's not what you grew up with, is like chalk squealing and screeching on a blackboard. Boring. Painful. Not to mention the emotional part that started to feel like manipulation when you were watching it from the outside.

I took notice. *I checked myself. Had I failed to lead my students to "get" the kind of singing they were experiencing? Were they mocking God? Were my kids unteachable?* No! I knew and loved these students. I'd been to their homes and knew their parents. Something else was going on. I began to look for other tools or ways of engaging God apart from singing. "Hey Lil, we sang 'my glorious' 81 times!" rang in my head for months afterward.

But even before this, I was hearing and reading about things happening "across the pond." I read an article about some youth leaders and young adults working in the Anglican Church in the UK, experimenting with all sorts of creative ways to tell God's story. These leaders were tired of seeing under-30 year olds leave the church—or never even arriving. So they designed worship services using artistic expression, creative prayer exercises, technology, and multi-sensory interaction. This resonated so much with me that I decided I needed to go to England to take a look for myself.

Around the same time I attended the Youth Specialties' National Youth Workers Convention and took Mike Yaconelli's "Sabbath" critical concerns course. I experienced a prayer path and a prayer room for the first time. Let's just say I'd found my home.

I went to England in the summer of 2001 to check out the alternative worship scene and to see how we might adapt experiential worship for our students at Christ Church Glendale.

When I got back from England, my students and I spent 40 days planning a new worship service together. What resulted was an alternative worship service held on Sunday nights called "Sacred Space." It began as a youth service but quickly morphed to include students and people ranging from a four-year-old to a retired priest in his 70s.

So I've come a long way from just singing songs and leading a Bible study. And don't get me wrong: While I'm still totally passionate about teaching the Bible, I cannot go back to ordinary Bible lecturing. When I teach the Bible now, I engage students' multiple senses and leave room for group responses and participation—they're not just listening to me talk. I don't "lead" worship anymore; I now "curate" worship.

Curate, you ask? (I knew you would!) My friend Mark Pierson from New Zealand introduced me to the term. Just think of an art curator who selects the paintings and other artwork for a particular show or exhibit, and then hangs and arranges the artwork so it has meaning and creative presence. It's the job of the worship curator to bring all the pieces of the worship service/gathering together. It means helping people find their gifts and enabling them to share these gifts within the worship gathering and within the worshiping community. The sermon became the Prayer Stations in Sacred Space, and then we expanded this to create special worship events called Prayer Experiences. As the curator of worship, I have the great privilege of helping others learn to create experiential worship and get outside the worship box. (I train leaders and help churches all over the country learn how to engage emerging worship in their contexts—contact me with your questions at lillylewin@gmail.com.)

And to reinforce the power of nonverbal communication and interaction, let me share this: I recently did a workshop on experiential worship for the Cincinnati Women's Club. The majority of the women were in their 60s. I had two women in their 80s come up after and tell me stories from their childhood Sunday school experiences. They remembered vividly and could tell me the meanings of object lessons they had done! Talk about making a point that *sticks*. We remember what we do—curate a worship service rather than lead it.

Dan's Journey

Being a youth pastor with several hundred high schoolers in a large, conservative, evangelical Bible church was definitely an environment where preaching was the primary form of learning and communicating the Bible. So, I taught and preached the Bible to our youth the same way they did in the main church. At that time the larger, programmed youth meetings were all the rage in youth ministry, so we jumped in and provided a rock-pop band for worship and threw in some videos. Ours were primarily youth meetings where they'd come in, sit in their seats, sing a few songs, maybe watch a drama skit or video, listen to a 20- to 30-minute sermon, then sing a song to close the time. God actually did use these meetings, but I began to sense that maybe something wasn't quite right.

The more I studied church history, and the more I studied various ways the church has worshiped over the years, the more I realized our contemporary formats of worship gatherings aren't the only way the church has met. In spite of the fact that I couldn't find any worship format prescribed in the Bible, I certainly felt locked into "this is what a worship gathering looks like" as if it were by divine decree.

Soon I began asking questions:

- Where in the Bible does it say that when we gather for worship we're supposed to do a few songs, watch a video, listen to a message, and sing a closing song?
- Where did we get this meeting model?
- What is biblical worship? Is it primarily singing as most youth would define it?
- Where in the Bible does any sermon look even remotely like the ones we are taught to give in our churches today?
- How long do youth actually retain what we teach them?
- Why do we set up the room in rows of chairs staring at a stage when in the Bible it seemed they met in homes and probably had a whole different type of meeting setup?
- What about the youth who aren't into "singing" so many songs and cheering after each one? (A little self-disclosure: I was one of those non-singing, non-cheering types myself, yet we used to do that in our youth ministry anyway.)

At the time I didn't think anyone else was asking these questions, but it turns out that many people, like Lilly, were feeling the same way and asking these questions, too. So I began making some changes in our youth ministry and young adult ministry.

After the sermon ended we started encouraging people to go to "stations" so they could pray about what they'd just heard in the sermon. (Prior to that we normally would only play a song or two after the sermon and end the meeting. But as we gave permission for people to physically go somewhere and pray about the teaching, it was amazing to see the response.)

We then put together more creative Prayer Stations that directly tied in with the teaching. (You'll read exactly how to put them together yourself in these pages.)

It wasn't easy to convince the church's leadership to initially allow these changes. Imagine being in a conservative Bible church and using interactive Prayer Stations instead of just sitting and listening to a Bible sermon. Students were behind a curtain in a "Chill Space" journaling their prayers. I preached while people in the room were creating interpretive paintings of the message. I remember the look on an elder's face as he asked, "Why are you buying incense?" Some wondered if we were sacrificing the Word of God for "experiences." We weren't—in fact, we were teaching the Scriptures in a way that allowed students to learn more, remember more, and pray more about what they'd learned. We still had teaching every single week. But we were adding prayer station responses and other ways to worship in the gatherings in addition to singing. I did have to back up what we were doing with Scripture and also show the practical, cultural reasons for our new teaching and worship methods. But it wasn't too hard—the Bible is filled with examples of teaching and worship using a multitude of forms.

Chapter 4

"So, How Do I Do This?"
The Power of Story and the Experiential Process

Stories invite us into a world other than ourselves. And, if they are good and true stories, they invite us into a world larger than ourselves. Bible stories are good and true stories, and the world that they invite us into is the world of God's creation and salvation and blessing.

—Eugene Peterson, *Subversive Spirituality*

Experiential worship is not about being in the "audience"; it's about being **a participant in the story**. Experiential worship involves corporate participation as well as individual participation. Participation enables us to "get" the story faster than anything else.

Plus, as the Holy Spirit is teaching, and as the students participate, "leaders" are set free from being the "experts." In experiential worship, we all learn together. That doesn't mean you throw out studying or preparation; it just means the information is no longer delivered by a talking head; instead the information is delivered through hands-on, sensory experiences. The message is *participated* in, not just listened to.

Let's look at the experiential process.

(And remember that this is a *group* process; the more people you involve as you begin integrating experiential worship into your context, the more gifts, creativity, ideas, and inspiration will emerge.)

1. *Choose your topic or Scripture passage.* Some folks begin with a topic, theme, or even an object—then incorporate Scripture to illustrate the subject. Or you can simply use a Scripture passage itself.

2. *Read the text yourself and with your group/leaders/team.* Read the passage from more than one translation so you can absorb various nuances and observe it unfolding in different ways.

3. *Try reading the Scripture several times, slowly, listening to what's in the passage and allowing the Holy Spirit to highlight things for you.* Those are the initial steps in the prayer exercise of *Lectio Divina*, in which you'd also focus on a single word or phrase you're drawn to and then spend time praying and asking God how you should respond.

4. *Do a background check on the passage and really study it.* Study commentaries; know the context of the passage. The worship creation process can be a Bible study for you and your creative team. (You may want to ask someone who enjoys getting into the meat of biblical passages to do this; it doesn't have to be you, the leader.)

5. *What sensory experiences are occurring in the text/passage?* What sights, sounds, smells, etc., can you extract from the passage? What colors do you see? Who is acting or reacting in the story? Make a list of these things.

6. *Begin with the end in mind.* What do you want participants to take away from the passage/lesson/experience? This is KEY. Ask the "So what?" question. What point is the passage making?

7. *Another question to ask:* "What *don't* they get?" What problems, fears, or doubts might this message or passage stir up within them?

8. *What objects (that you use NOW) can enhance the story?* What will they see again later to remind them of the story?

9. *What is your purpose?* Are you creating this Prayer Station to enhance your message, or is the Prayer Station itself the message? How do you want participants to respond to and/or interact with the text? Will they respond as a group or individually?

10. *Now start thinking about music.* Think outside the box of Christian choruses or the usual Christian music fare. Consider old hymns performed in new ways; consider popular songs on the radio/iTunes at the moment that might fit. (It'll really help to harness the knowledge of a student who's really up to speed with popular music—especially among teenagers—to help here.) Make a song list.

11. *If you don't have a worship band, you can have someone create a "backdrop" CD or iPod playlist instead.* You also can choose not to have singing at all during the worship gathering and just have backdrop/ambient music. Or you might try using a CD for the majority of the worship time and then close with a corporately sung song. This can educate your group about different ways to worship and give your music team the opportunity to engage God in a new way, too.

12. *Assign tasks.* Experiential worship isn't a solo performance. It's best created in community—a team process. (See "Chapter 4: Building Your Team") Think about what needs doing: Writing and creating signs for different stations, getting props, setting up the room/space, cleaning

up/tearing down the space, readings to be written or assigned, getting the music together, creating slides/video/PowerPoint, gathering or creating art, setting up the stations themselves…

(*Note*: Writing the text for the signs/directions to follow for Prayer Stations is sometimes the most time-consuming task. I actually started with handwritten signage, but it's really great to have them on computer so they can be used again or reworked in new ways for future worship—which is what we provide on the CD that accompanies this book!)

13. *Consider your group's makeup.* Who's in your community? What's the age range? What's the group's personality? Does your group need lots of direction or only a little to get in the mood for quieting minds and hearts to pray?

14. *Consider your group's size.* The number of people in your group will determine the number of stations you need to create—or, if you have a larger number of folks, you may need to replicate the stations (e.g., repeating three or four stations in various parts of the room/worship area/gathering space). The size of your group and your worship space will determine the amount of supplies you need and may limit how much movement you can allow.

15. *Consider your environment.* Where will you be setting up your Prayer Stations or Prayer Experiences? What is the size of your room? What are the natural spaces/areas where a Prayer Station will fit? What are the negatives about this space? Think about the things that might detract from worship, such as a lit-up soda or candy machine, bright lights that cannot be turned down, or spaces next door to yours that may bring a lot of noise into your environment. You want a space conducive to prayer and reflection—silence, solitude, rest, a place to be with and engage with God.

Let's give the process a try by creating a response or two from a passage of Scripture.

Take it step by step using Luke 5:1-11 (the calling of the first disciples) and the 15 questions/tasks just described. Go and do it and come back when you're finished. (Just remember your high school English class and write down the who, what, when, where, and why of the passage. Don't assume that anyone knows anything about the story! Start thinking visually. Start thinking symbolically.)

All done? Okay, here's what we came up with:

What are the sights, sounds, smells, tastes, objects in this passage? *The water, the beach, fishing nets, the smell of fish, the taste of salt in the air, a crowd of people eager to hear Jesus, two fishing boats, fishermen. The noise of the crowd, the sound of Jesus' voice, the sound of waves against the shore, maybe seagulls crying.*

What are the natural elements, colors? *Blue sky, perhaps clouds and sunshine, the colors of various garments people are wearing. The colors of gray or brown in the sand and rocks along the shore; the blue, green, gray color of the sea itself.*

Who are the people, the actors in the story? *Jesus, the crowd, Simon, the other fishermen. Don't forget that not everyone will know that Simon is also called Peter and his brother is Andrew. (Refer back to Matthew 4:18-22.) So Andrew is probably there, too.*

Now let's answer the English-class questions:

Who? *Jesus, Simon (Peter), Andrew, large crowd of people, James, and John.*

What? *Jesus is teaching at the seaside. Simon and the boys are cleaning their nets after fishing all night.*

When? *Daytime (probably morning because they talk about fishing all night, and it's before Jesus has selected his disciples).*

Where? *On the beach beside the Lake of Gennesaret, which is the Sea of Galilee, and on the sea itself.*

Why is this important? *It's actually the calling of Jesus' first disciples. It's the passage where Peter, Andrew, James, and John are invited to follow Jesus, to leave fishing to become fishers of people. That's big stuff!*

So does this passage raise any questions for you, just off the top of your head? *What would it mean for them to leave their jobs and follow Jesus? What would Peter think when a rabbi and carpenter's son tells him, a professional fisherman, that he should fish in the deep water in the middle of the day—the worst time for fishing? If I were Peter, would I have listened and obeyed? Or would I have said, "Forget it!"?*

Other observations from reading the passage? *After the huge catch of fish, Peter realizes that Jesus is holy, and that he isn't worthy to be with Jesus, yet Jesus doesn't go away when Peter asks him to. Instead, Jesus invites Peter to be his follower.*

So…what do I want to focus on, and what do I want my community, my students, to take away from this passage? We created a Prayer Station about our fears of following Jesus. We asked what it would take for each of us to get out of the boat, leave our nets, and follow him. What would it take for us to leave our comfort zones and actually become a Jesus follower? So we placed an inflatable boat in the center of our worship space and taped the signs/directions to the sides of it. Each person actually took turns standing in the boat and praying.

What other station ideas come to mind? The net filled with fish inspired awe in these fishermen. They knew it was a miracle because they'd fished all night and caught nothing, and now here was an extravagant catch in broad daylight. You might have people look at a net filled with fish (play fish or paper fish) or a photo of a net filled with fish and ask what would inspire them to know that a miracle had happened (i.e., what would Jesus do to inspire them to see miracles in their everyday lives?).

You might also have an opportunity for your students to confess their sins. Peter realizes he's a sinful man, not worthy to be in the presence of Jesus. They could write their confessions on a fish and leave these in the boat or perhaps place them in another net at the foot of a cross.

You could have photos of the sea, the beach, or other fishing boats on a screen. You could even create a beach with real sand on which people could sit and think about what it'd be like to listen to Jesus teach and preach, to actually have been in that crowd at the Sea of Galilee. You could use beach or sea sounds in your backdrop CD. (Once we created a station where we set up some photos of the beach, put out a tarp with some sand on which participants sat, and had two or three CD players for them to listen to ocean sounds so they could picture Jesus at the beach with them and what he would say to them.)

So…instead of just having your kids listen to a talk on Luke 5:1-11, you've helped them *experience* Luke 5:1-11.

Chapter 5

Building Your Team

Building a team of people is so important because without many helping out, it's easy to burn out one or two who end up doing everything. And having burned out a leadership team by "building the plane and flying it at the same time," I don't recommend starting something without counting the cost and taking time to plan ahead and prepare your team and your worshiping community.

The goal is to create a team that works with the leader/facilitator/curator to enhance all aspects of the worship gathering. This team can consist of people of all ages, not just youth/students. You never know who might have the photography or videography or tech gift among you. The team goes through the experiential process from chapter 4, or one you create that works for your community/youth group.

The "Palette Team" Approach

At Vintage Faith Church the creative team is called the Palette Team. These creative folks meet once a month to brainstorm ideas and plan for upcoming messages. Dan says it's his favorite meeting of the month because they actually experience creativity together and share ideas and participate in an exercise or Prayer Experience that relates to the upcoming themes.

The palette metaphor describes a group of people who oversee specific areas of creativity (music, fine art, spoken word, teaching, prayer stations, etc.). Each of the Palette Team members represents a "color" who together "paint" a worship gathering and what happens in it using a variety of creative expressions.

The way the Palette Team works is that Dan, the teacher, brings a printed handout listing the following month's teaching from week to week (subject, Scripture passages, and goals). The Palette Team gets the handout and walks through it together week by week. They try to get about a month ahead in planning, which causes less stress and more time to get ready. The Palette Team then meets with other teams to plan more things in detail.

These people may not enjoy all the creative processes and non-linear thinking, but you can't make a weekly service run smoothly without them:

- **Administrators** (paperwork; communications pieces).
- **Setup/clean up** folks to help put together the space and tear it down. If new people want to get involved, this is a great team for them. Most people are willing to help if they're invited to and asked sincerely. You may even want to ask those who are very skeptical of the whole "new worship stuff."
- **Welcome and hospitality.** Prayer Stations and Prayer Experiences need welcome people/greeters just as church services do. These folks will help people know what to do once they get there.

(*Note*: The gift of hospitality is one of the biggest banners we can fly that says we're followers of Jesus. How we welcome and serve others and make them feel at home and loved says tons, no matter where they are on their faith journeys—but especially to folks seeking to know God. Therefore these welcome and hospitality folks are vital to the prayer and worship experiences. But please make sure they truly have "the gift." It helps if they're extroverts with a history of encouraging newcomers and folks on the fringe to get involved.)

Building a Team Will Take Time

It takes time to develop relationships with people and build trust among the group. Don't view this as a quick, easy process—it may take many months. Allow for this time and the space to grow as a creative community. Sharing ideas and creativity is sometimes risky. *Practice.* Leave room to fail. Remind people to honor each other and all ideas. (Remember—when you brainstorm, there are no "bad" ideas.) Most importantly, have fun as you create.

Getting Started

Are you willing to make the commitment to give this a try? Begin by starting the conversation with potential members of your team. Show them examples in this book. You'll discern where you are in getting the experiential process off the ground based on where they are and how they respond. You may not be ready for a full-blown worship service or worship experience, but as you put together your team and discover the gifts and talents of those in your group/ community, you'll be able to gauge the interest and the opportunity.

So don't get discouraged—just start with baby steps.

Chapter 6

Baby Steps

When we started creating worship beyond preaching and singing, we didn't jump in and do full-blown Prayer Experiences all at once. It was a little-by-little process of starting small and building a team. Here's what we suggest:

1. *Start small and think "simple."* Add a station or an experiential element to your regular worship/teaching time. Add experiential, interactive learning to your lesson, Bible study, sermon, prayer time, etc. Then add two or three stations.

2. *Think about people who might join you in this process.* Who would be interested in being a part of the creative team and the creative process? Start praying for these folks. These are volunteers who will share their gifts and bring their creativity to worship.

3. *Art stations.* You might start by just putting a table with art supplies in your gathering/worship space. Provide various types of paper, pens, markers, colored pencils, sketchpads, oils, chalk, and pastels so those who like to draw, doodle, sketch, etc., can use them during a talk. Announce that the art supplies are there to be used during worship time and then invite students to try them. You can also pass out paper and pens to your entire group and ask participants to sketch or draw or write about what strikes them regarding your talk—and just see what they come up with. These can be displayed as part of worship, if desired.

4. *Start a collection.* Begin to gather the elements you'll need to create Prayer Stations and a Sacred Space environment. Do you have a storeroom or a basement at your church where stuff gets stashed and gathers dust for years? Take a trip to that place and look at the treasures. Are there candleholders, tables, or old stuff from ages past that no one has seen in, well, forever? After you get permission to use this stuff, ask yourself how you could reinvent these things. Next, try your own attic or basement. Better yet, try your parents' or even grandparents' attics and basements. Almost anything can be an inspiration for a worship station.

For example, a small group of middle schoolers can create a Prayer Station using a collection of old shoeboxes formed into a cross and spray- painted black.

So start collecting old candlesticks, crosses, manger scenes, stars, crowns, treasure chests, etc. Check out stores such as Hobby Lobby, Michaels, Cost Plus World Market, Party City, Pier 1 Imports, and the Dollar Tree. (Dollar stores are great!) Go to flea markets, yard sales, garage sales, tag sales. Check out craigslist, Freecycle, and other online clearinghouses for stuff folks want to give away. Ask others if they have stuff you need (which involves that dreaded planning ahead); many have candles, fabric, and plastic tablecloths lying around their houses that they'd love to donate. Find people with the gift of acquisition—folks who like to go to tag sales and yard sales and are willing to be on the lookout for worship gear and worship elements.

You don't have to have big budgets or be a big church to do this. Don't feel like you have to have all the latest technology, either.

Experiential worship can be done low-tech as well as high-tech.

5. *Pray.* Ask Jesus what his plans are…and ask him to prepare the hearts of your leadership to be willing to try new things—perhaps even stuff way outside their comfort zones. *Then, pray again!* Pray over the process as you create and plan and pray over the room as you set up and tear down your worship space.

6. *Take your group through the experiential worship process in order to whet their appetites and get them interested in creating it.*

7. *Remember that the God of creation is at work*—and the action of creating Prayer Stations and experiential elements is an act of worship in itself. Jesus is always the central focus of what we do and why we do it.

8. *Don't force change in existing adult worship gatherings at your church.* We assume you'll use this book primarily to design worship gathering for youth and young adults. But if you ever get the chance to lead or add to the adult main worship gatherings, honor the heritage. Be considerate of the way people are used to worshiping. However, if the senior pastor or leadership allows you to experiment in the adult gathering, you'll find that adults, not just youth, connect with experiential worship.

Chapter 7

Helpful Hints for Experiential Worship/Prayer Station Setup

Become an Atmosphere Architect

You don't have to be an artist yourself to create Sacred Spaces or experiential worship, but it's an opportunity for you to discover those in your community who are. It's also an opportunity for you to become the atmosphere architect of your worship time and worship space.

"Atmosphere Architecture" is the phrase author Steve Sjogren uses to describe the creation of the entire room—the total environment. *How does the worship space feel as you enter? The music, the lighting, the vibe in the space? Can you create the vibe from the entrance—from the time they walk in the building or as they near your worship space? What can you do to get people ready for worship?*

How does the room look, smell, feel? What you see when you walk in tells you what to expect. It also communicates loudly that you were expecting people. The Atmosphere Architecture of the room sets the vibe and tone for worship: *Is it peaceful and worshipful? Or chaotic and disorganized?* Think about what vibe you want to communicate. *What things can you do to create a vibe that relates to your worship design and theme?*

Find people who do this naturally. Find people who are good at lighting and decor. Find people who "get" the vibe and can help create it.

Music affects the vibe of your worship and the Atmosphere Architecture. Get someone who's into music to create a "backdrop" (i.e., background) CD or iPod playlist for your Prayer Experience or worship service. (This is different from a set of worship songs because the backdrop songs enhance the theme of the station or experience; they're not intended to sing along to.)

Placing Prayer Stations in the Room.

In Dan's church, there are sermons each week. So prayer stations are set up to the side so they aren't a distraction—and so people aren't in full view of others when they pray. This allows a bit more privacy. The teacher normally ends the message by explaining the prayer station, then the worship band plays more music, and students can make their way to the stations. Lilly uses lots of variety in how content is communicated. Often she has only ambient music playing for atmosphere, then has the group manage prayer stations, and then has a discussion rather than a message. So the stations can either be in the center—and the focus of the meeting—or along the outside of the room.

After your stations are set up, always have someone read through the signs at each station to make sure they make sense and are in order. (You want to catch things that might confuse participants *before* the experience begins!) Also, you might have someone show participants an example of a response to a station before the experience starts. Participants will then know what to do, and this also gives them permission to participate at each station.

When the Experience Starts.

As you begin a Prayer Experience or time of worship, always remind participants to slow down and read the signs…to actually participate in the experience…not just race through so that they can say they're "done." Give them permission to take their time and remind them that this their time to be alone with God—not to be a group.

Table Coverings

1. *Keep the table coverings consistent.* This will help your stations look clean, and the whole experience will fit together. Start a collection of canvas tarps/drop cloths for your base table coverings. These painter's drop cloths come in various sizes and can be purchased at Lowes or The Home Depot.

Other table coverings we've used include plastic tablecloths in various colors. These can be reused, and they come in round and rectangular shapes. Black is my favorite color for them. You can start a collection of sheets and tablecloths in various colors; I prefer white or cream. Advertise this need to your whole congregation; as people clean out closets or prepare to move, you'll get some great stuff.

2. *Keep a theme going with colors.* Start a collection of solid-colored fabric pieces. Have someone scout discount stores for remnants and sales. A friend of Lilly's inherited an entire closet of fabric bolts when one of their church members cleaned house! Dan's crew at Vintage Faith collected tapestry fabrics from yard sales and flea markets to use and reuse for station backdrops. Swatches of cloth or even colored wrapping paper on a station add to its beauty and interest.

You might want to check out the colors of the church year and collect fabrics in these colors.

- Purple or royal blue for Advent
- White or gold for Christmas and Epiphany
- Purple for Holy Week
- Black for Good Friday
- White or gold for Easter
- Red for Pentecost
- Green for the weeks following Pentecost (a.k.a., Ordinary Time)

Bases for Prayer Stations

When setting up a room for a Prayer Experience or experiential worship, look around for what's readily available to use for Prayer Stations. What tables, chairs, shelving units, and other "base" materials are around the room or near the room you'll be using for worship? Don't be bound by tables, either—anything can be used to create a worship station. Also don't be afraid to go outside your space. We would often set up the theme for our worship by introducing it in the hallway or exterior entrance to our worship space. We also set up Prayer Stations in the hallways and classrooms near the chapel since the chapel itself was rather small. Also, we used a courtyard to create stations when the weather was nice.

Signs/Directions

When we first began, most of our signs were handwritten. Since we now replicate many of our Prayer Stations and experiences, our signs are saved on computer so they're easily tweaked, altered, and printed out. I (Lilly) prefer large print so participants actually read the signs—and so more people can read them simultaneously. You may prefer smaller signs with logos that carry through the theme of the stations.

Be creative. Sometimes you'll want to use a combination of signs, some artistically designed and some plain or printed. The following are some suggestions for hanging and placing signs at stations:

- Plastic frames and sign holders can be purchased in bulk (try Staples and online vendors).
- Restaurant supply stores carry menu stands that also work well (also found online).
- Regular picture frames are great. Just tape the signs on the outside, don't bother trying to put the signs inside the frame. We found some nice ones at our local dollar store and reuse them.

- Blue painter's tape. When hanging signs on walls and furniture, use this tape whenever possible. (You'll save a lot of explaining and re-painting!) If you're creating a Prayer Room or Prayer Experience that will go on for more than one day, test your tape. You may need to use a sturdier tape so your signs and posters don't fall off the wall due to temperature changes over time. Also check wall types. Certain wall coverings don't hold tape at all—or require a special kind. Test ahead of time whenever possible.

Using Scent

Smell can be the hardest sense to engage in worship, but it's also the most powerful—especially when it comes to remembering it. At Sacred Space we use different scents for different seasons. We use a scented candle for Advent, another for Epiphany, and a different scented candle...more mossy and earthy...for Lent. I've learned the hard way that you *don't want to use too much scent or too many scented candles for worship.* People with allergies and asthma can be hurt by such scents, to say nothing of the fact that worship is disrupted instead of enhanced.

So try one or two candles with the same scent and use unscented candles for the rest so you don't, um, stink up the experience. You might experiment with scent according to the size of your worship space/room and the number of people in your group. A scented candle that greets folks as they enter your space helps create a mood, but beware of mixing scents (using more than one scent) in a room—this can cause nausea.

Lighting

Candles are always a great way to add mood to a room, but always use candles in jars or with some kind of glass holder around them. Some buildings don't allow candles at all (for fear of fire or messing up the carpeting), so we've gotten creative and used rope lighting—i.e., small white Christmas lights—and started collecting other lighting strands with themes. Rope lighting is great for highlighting stations and creating pathways. You can find strand or rope lighting at stores such as Target, Hobby Lobby, or Michaels.

Indirect lighting can also be powerful. You can purchase workman's spotlights (the silver kind that clip on objects) at hardware stores.

Specific Stations

Wailing Wall. The majority of Prayer Experiences and Prayer Rooms that we create include a Wailing Wall station. This is a wall covered in large butcher paper where participants can write their prayers and heart cries to God. It's amazing the deeply felt, intimate prayers that students will share on the Wall—things they would never share out loud, even with their friends.

(*Note*: Always treat the completed Wailing Wall with great respect. It contains the private prayers of your students, so keep them that way and dispose of the "wall" after the Prayer Room/Prayer Experience has ended. You might have some of your leaders pray over the wall during the course of the Prayer Experience time, praying for the needs and requests written and depicted on it.)

Offer a global perspective whenever possible. Give your group the opportunity to pray for the needs of our world—not just the United States of America. Set up Prayer Stations that cover global needs, with maps, information on missionaries, worldwide news, features on crisis areas, etc. Allow participants to pray for these places and events and encourage them to pray daily for our country and our world.

Include opportunities for confession/repentance. We talk a lot about Jesus forgiving our sins, but how often do we give our students the opportunity to actually repent and give these sins to Jesus? When creating a Prayer Experience, we always design a station within it that gives participants the opportunity to confess and repent.

What *Not* to Do When Leading/Organizing a Prayer Room

If you're creating a Prayer Room for a specific time period or for a retreat or conference, here are a few things to remember.

1. *Don't dictate time.* The participants, especially students, need to be able to spend as much time or as little, as they want to.

2. *No vocal music should be heard in the Prayer Room.* The backdrop music should be instrumental and soothing. Like a spa…relaxing. As participants enter the Prayer Room, they should feel the quiet relaxation of the space. The vibe must be peaceful, not loud.

3. *Quiet is the only real rule.* This time is for each person to be with God. It's not a time for socializing or dialogue. (You could set aside an additional room or space for conversation and group prayer. Things often come up as students experience the Prayer Room, so you may have folks available to pray with or talk to participants. This is an additional opportunity, however, and should not distract the rest of the pray-ers from their one-on-one time with Jesus.)

4. *Don't skimp on hosts for your Prayer Room/Prayer Experience.* Hosts are important! These people can welcome participants as they enter the Prayer Room and help them get started if they need instruction. They're also responsible for refilling any "take aways" from stations and

making sure that candles are safely used. This person can hang art prayers at the art station as they collect and straighten up any station that may need it in the course of a Prayer-Room time.

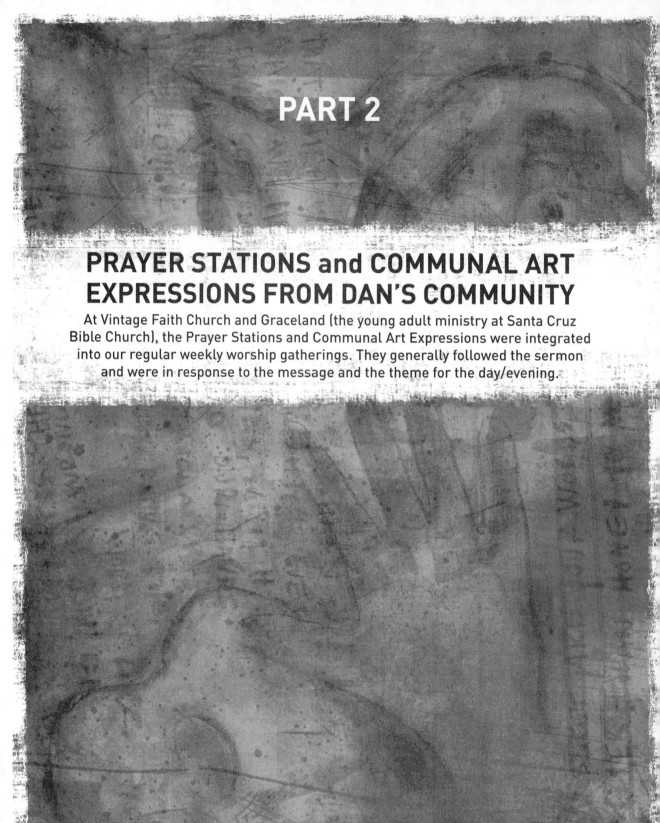

PART 2

PRAYER STATIONS and COMMUNAL ART EXPRESSIONS FROM DAN'S COMMUNITY

At Vintage Faith Church and Graceland (the young adult ministry at Santa Cruz Bible Church), the Prayer Stations and Communal Art Expressions were integrated into our regular weekly worship gatherings. They generally followed the sermon and were in response to the message and the theme for the day/evening.

BE THE CHURCH

1 Communal Art Expression; 3 Prayer Stations

The word *church* was first spoken by Jesus himself in Matthew 16:18-19 when he was physically standing in a place in Israel called "The Gates of Hades," which was thought to be the entrance to hell itself and where many gods were worshiped in niches in the rocks. At this important spiritual location, Jesus introduced the word *church* for the first time. His church will be built upon a rock (the same metaphor used in Matthew 7:24-29) and nothing can keep it from standing interminably.

Unfortunately, the idea of church has drifted from being a supernatural community of faith (i.e., an organism made up of many individuals who are unique but with a common denominator of each being the church) to being a label for a building on a city map or a time slot on some people's calendars (or a time slot intentionally avoided by many).

Teaching: This teaching focus allows students to look into New Testament Scripture passages that flesh out what it looks like to be the church Jesus dreamed of and dreams of still. Many passages from the Old Testament also apply to this topic, since being the church is really about an evident lifestyle of relationship with God.

Be the Church: "I Dream of a Church…"

Scripture: 1 Corinthians 12; Romans 12:4-6

Themes: Mission, Spiritual Gifts, the Church, Character

Purpose: This Communal Art Expression addresses what it means to be a community of Jesus' followers. It ties into the New Testament metaphor of the church community being like a human body with many different functions and faculties of motion.

Activity/Response: Students will take time to write out specifically what they dream Jesus' church could be. They can each visit tables around the room to grab a card and a pen, they can each receive a card upon entering the gathering, or the cards can be placed underneath their chairs before they enter the room.

They will complete the sentence: "I dream of a church…" After they each write their dreams, they go to the designated wall space and tape or tack their cards on the wall along with the other participants.

After this time of response, a facilitator can wrap up the Communal Art Expression time with a prayer and possibly by reading some of the dreams posted around the room—asking God to continue building the church using each individual in the room and millions around the world.

Supplies:
- Tables and tablecloths or tapestries
- Blank 3 x 5 cards or squares of paper
- 20 to 50 pens
- Tape or thumb tacks (depending on your surface)
- Boxes or baskets (as needed)

Setting Up the Stations: (Optional) Decorate tables around the room for students to visit, putting cards and pens in baskets for easy accessibility. Place tape or thumb tacks in baskets in several places near the wall where students will post the cards.

Signs/Directions: None necessary; verbal instructions should be sufficient.

Be the Church: Using Our Gifts

Scripture: 1 Corinthians 12; Romans 12:4-6

Themes: Mission, Spiritual Gifts, the Church

Purpose: This Prayer Station addresses what it means to be a community of Jesus' followers. It ties into the New Testament metaphor of the church community being like a human body with many different functions and faculties of motion.

Activity/Response: Students will take sticky notes out of the gift box or basket, writing on them one of the gifts they believe is theirs, given to them by God. They will place the sticky notes on the butcher paper cutout of a human body, prayerfully dedicating their gifts for the good of others on the mission of the church.

Supplies:
- Table and tablecloth or tapestries
- Instructional signs on 8.5 x 11 paper
- 2 or 3 candles
- A box or basket with gift-wrapping or a bow
- Sticky notes (as needed)
- 4 to 6 pens
- Scissors and butcher paper to create the human body shape

Setting Up the Station: Place a tablecloth on the table—and put the instructional signs and Scripture passage(s) in multiple places where they can be easily read. Cut out a giant piece of butcher paper in the shape of a human body (an artist in your community could freehand it, or you could use someone as a template, having the person lay on his back and tracing around him). Wrap the box or place a bow on the basket. Place the sticky notes in the box or basket. Put the pens in an accessible place.

Signs/Directions: On accompanying CD

Be the Church: Community

Scripture: 1 Corinthians 12; Romans 12:4-6; 1 John 4:12

Themes: Mission, Spiritual Gifts, the Church, Community/Fellowship

Purpose: This Prayer Station addresses what it means to be a community of Jesus' followers. It ties into the New Testament metaphor of the church community being like a human body with many different functions and faculties of motion.

Teaching: This specific Prayer Station on the topic of "Being the Church" addresses how beautiful it is to be together in community when we're on the mission as the church—sharing life with each other as followers of Jesus and being with each other when life's difficulties present themselves. You may want to have students from your community share about how the church has been that community in their lives.

After the Teaching: After the teaching, time is given (with live or recorded music) for students to interact with the Prayer Stations that directly tie into what was just taught. It's always important to walk through the instructions well, helping the students see the symbolism and the prayer focus that tie in to the teaching.

Activity/Response: As students approach the Prayer Station, instructions (see sign text on accompanying CD) are given to students to read, as well as the corresponding Scripture passage. More than one student can participate at this station at a time.

Students enter the tent, spending some time in prayer and reflection. The students can help themselves to tea. As they're sitting down, reading Scripture passages and the displayed signs, they're invited to prayerfully consider what God intends community to be and dialog with God about their fears, hopes, and concerns.

Supplies:
- Tapestries and pillows for the floor
- Instructional signs on 8.5 x 11 paper
- Floor lamps or clip-on desk lamps
- Thermoses filled with hot water and a basket of assorted teas
- Cookies (optional)

- Paint or markers to create the one-word signs
- Scripture passages and theme signs on 8.5 x 11 paper
- Material for setting up a giant tent

Setting Up the Station: Set up the tent (you could use a large canopy with mosquito netting on either side, or you could use several small tents—each illustrating a different aspect of how community is a place of comfort in our lives on the mission) with inside lighting. Put the instructional signs and Scripture passages in multiple places where they can be easily read. Arrange pillows and tapestries comfortably for students to sit on. Decorate the space with a few art pieces or crosses if you want. Place words around (printed or painted on 8½ x 11 papers, or larger if desired) for contemplation: The words are *authenticity, encouragement, share, sorrow, Scripture, life, celebrate*. Provide hot water in thermoses with a basket of teas (and cookies if desired), with adequate signage inviting the students to help themselves.

Signs/Directions: On accompanying CD

Be the Church: Communion

Scripture: Matthew 26:17-30; Colossians 1:15-23; 1 Corinthians 12; Romans 12:4-6

Themes: Mission, the Church, Scripture/Theology, Worship, Community/Fellowship

Purpose: This Prayer Station helps focus students' attention on their roles as worshipers of God—completely acknowledging God as Lord and Redeemer as they give themselves to God's way and truth.

Teaching: This specific Prayer Station on the topic of "Being the Church" addresses the importance of worship and humble acknowledgment of God's greatness. If we claim to follow Jesus, we must be people of reflection—those who meditate on the life and person and way of Jesus as we seek to imitate him. As we participate in this ancient celebration (Communion), we, too, like the physical body of Christ, are spiritually sent out for others to "taste" who Jesus is by our lifestyles.

Activity/Response: This Prayer Station simply allows students to take Communion with a special focus of prayer and consideration. Students are encouraged to take the cracker in hand and really think through the life of Jesus and the lives we are to live in his footsteps. As they dip the cracker in the grape juice, they're encouraged to reflect and worship.

Supplies:
- Table and tablecloth or tapestries
- Instructional signs and Scripture passages on 8.5 x 11 paper
- 2 or 3 candles
- Bread
- Dish for bread
- Grape juice (either in two big cups in which students can dip the bread or in small cups—one for each student—for the same purpose)

Setting Up the Station: Put the instructional signs and Scripture passages in multiple places where they can be easily read. Place the bread on a clean dish in small pieces. Put a glass of grape juice on either side of the station. Decorate the table with candles and tapestries as needed.

Signs/Directions: On accompanying CD

THE BEATITUDES

2 Communal Art Expressions

COMMUNAL ART EXPRESSION

The Beatitudes: The Light of Christ

Scripture: Matthew 5:14-16

Themes: Attitudes of the Heart, Authenticity, Purity, Mercy, Persecution, Living in the Kingdom, Evangelism

Purpose: This Communal Art Expression ties into the teaching of Jesus in the Sermon on the Mount about being the "light" of the world in Matthew 5:14-16

How to Use This Communal Art Expression: It's vitally important that a facilitator adequately instruct the group of students at the beginning of this communal art response. Take this visual opportunity to reinforce (with Scripture) that we are lights carrying the Light in our schools, workplaces, and relationships. Have students take out their candles from under their chairs or wherever they may be located. Explain that six students will approach the front of the room and light their candles, symbolic of welcoming the Light into their lives, and that everyone will be lighting each other's candles until every candle is lit. (Have the band or a few song leaders play two to three songs that will help students reflect and worship during the time their candles are lit.)

After this explanation, invite the six individuals to light their candles with the Light at the base of the cross. Assign each of the six a section of the room and have them walk to their assigned sections and light the candle of the first person in a row of seats (and that candle's flame is used to light another person's candle, etc.).

After everyone's candles are lit, have the facilitator return and lead the community in prayer before everyone blows their candles out.

Option: You could hand out the candles at a time when they won't be distracting, or you could decide to have the offering and offering prayer after the teaching, then have the ushers pass out the candles with the offering bag.

Supplies:
- Candle for every student (Overestimate! Better safe than sorry.)
- Large cross, centrally located
- Big candle for the base of the cross—a large pillar candle is a great choice

- Optional: Tapestries or fabric to drape around the cross
- Butcher paper or construction paper with paint or markers to paint the phrases "Jesus Is the Light" or "I Am the Light of the World—Jesus" on a sign for the cross

Setting Up the Station: Use the cross, big candle, and butcher-paper sign as a visual during the whole gathering. Distribute the candles. A group facilitator gives both the teaching tie-in to the expression and the instructions. Use appropriate music for the candle lighting. Close in prayer. (Check with the senior pastor in regard to fire safety policies before attempting this.)

Signs/Directions: None necessary; verbal instructions should be sufficient.

The Beatitudes: Paintings

Scripture: Matthew 5:3-12

Themes: Attitudes of the Heart, Authenticity, Purity, Mercy, Persecution, Living in the Kingdom

Purpose: It directly ties into Jesus' teaching of the Beatitudes in the Sermon on the Mount in Matthew 5:3-12.

Teaching: The teaching is to focus (over a series of weeks if possible) on each of Jesus' "Blessed are…" statements, which help us understand the nature and values of the Kingdom of God. Each of Jesus' statements is shocking and countercultural—both in its New Testament context and in our own. With every statement, Jesus redefines what is valuable—what attitudes and perspectives are to be sought and pursued by his followers. This passage, being the first of Jesus' teachings recorded in the Gospel of Matthew, is pivotal for our understanding of the actions and attitudes of the kingdom of heaven.

During the Teaching (over a span of weeks if possible): Invite eight students from your faith community who are gifted artists to participate in this. (*Note:* It's ideal to welcome artists of various styles and mediums. Most may use normal paints, but perhaps some employ nontraditional art forms, such as tattooing, woodworking, etc.)

Each artist is assigned a particular "Blessed are…" statement, and over the course of the weekly teaching series, they're each to work on their pieces incrementally. During the teaching portion of the gathering, these artists can be posted at lighted stations around the room, creating their artwork.

One requirement is that somewhere on the art piece, the corresponding Scripture passage is actually written out; there will be a lot of creative expressions of the Beatitudes, and the resulting art may not clearly depict which one it represents.

You may want to incorporate the Reader's Theater (see accompanying CD) into each teaching time to reinforce the power of the Beatitudes.

After the Teaching (the last night of the series): You may want to have this final night of the series be a summary of all the weeks, where each piece of art (each Beatitude) is highlighted.

You could even interview the individual artists (even if you choose to interview only one or two of them) to describe the meaning and symbolism of their representations of the passage.

After the summary teaching, adequate time is given (with live or recorded music playing) for students to go to each of the eight art stations, where they can interact with the art, pray, and consider the Scripture passage.

Activity/Response: Students approach each art station, and the first thing they see is the art piece displayed centrally and the Scripture passage and prayer focus written out large and dominant on two separate pieces of paper (see accompanying CD). Have several copies displayed so more than one student can participate at this station at a time.

Supplies:
DURING THE TEACHING:
- Adequate lighting for each artist station (an idea: desk lamps with clips attached on the easels or to the table top used)
- Stool or chair (according to the artist's preference)
- Any art supplies you can donate to the artist according to their individual needs
- Sheets or drop cloths under the artists' stations
- Butcher paper or construction paper with paint or markers to paint each "Blessed are…" passage for the artist to refer to and for students to see as they watch them painting during the teaching

AFTER THE TEACHING (for each table/station):
- Scripture passages and prayer focuses on 8.5 x 11 sheets of paper
- 2 or 3 candles for each table
- Tablecloth or tapestries to decorate each table
- Signs

Setting Up the Stations: Place a tablecloth on the table. Display the art piece centrally on a tabletop easel or raise it with books under tapestries. You may want to light it with a clip-on desk lamp. Place both the Scripture passage and the prayer focus sheets in multiple places so students can clearly read them and more than one student can participate at a time.

Signs/Directions: On accompanying CD

BELONGING

2 Communal Art Expressions

Purpose: These Communal Art Expressions can be used for any gathering focusing on community in general, the body of Christ metaphor, or our individual contributions to Jesus' church.

Teaching (general): Throughout God's interaction with humankind in history, God has defined us as individuals in relationship with himself and each other. We express our full selves when we are in relationships. We belong in relationships. Scripture is full of passages and allegories of how we can actively contribute to God's plan in the world and in each other's lives as the church through relationships. Mysteriously, our unique contribution has temporal *and* eternal effects. The artistic medium of the mosaic can illustrate how our brokenness can be joined with others as part of God's purpose and plan to express truth in an unexpectedly beautiful way.

Belonging: Mosaic

Scripture: 1 Corinthians 12; Ephesians 4; Romans 12

Themes: Purpose, Church, Salvation, Identity, Mission

Note: This Communal Art Expression is most effective when used over several weeks of gatherings. If it's truly used as a hands-on prayer and worship opportunity in conjunction with teaching, it can be a response option several weeks in a row.

How to Use This Communal Art Expression: It's important to have an artist in your community (perhaps even a contractor) assist with this project logistically. This is essentially a mosaic designed for long-term display. An artist should first draw the body images on a piece of board. In the gathering, each student will choose a piece of broken glass or pottery. (Make sure the sharp edges have been smoothed out enough that cuts won't happen.)

You may want to divide the image into several sections so there can be multiple tables around the room for students to visit (e.g., one with the legs, one with the center of the body, one with the head, and two with an arm each). A facilitator should be present at each table to apply the mosaic adhesive on the spot of board each student chooses. The student will then press the glass or pottery onto the board. An artist will probably have to wrap up the project, filling in with grout and other pieces as necessary. A contractor may help construct a stand to support the weight of this mosaic piece.

Supplies:
- Tables and tapestries or tablecloths
- Mosaic or tile grout
- Broken and colorful pieces of pottery or glass of various sizes
- Tile adhesive (found at your local home improvement store) and application paddle/brush
- Baseboard(s)
- Decorative wood for edging or for a stand (as needed)
- Protective gloves for each facilitator

Setting Up the Station: Decorate the table with tapestries. Place the board in the center of the table. Each facilitator should wear gloves, hold a paddle or brush for the adhesive, and continually lay out pieces of pottery and glass.

Signs/Directions: None necessary; verbal instructions should be sufficient.

Belonging: Speaking the Truth

Scripture: Romans 12:1-2; 1 Corinthians 12:27; Galatians 6:1-2; Ephesians 4:2-16

Themes: Purpose, Church, Salvation, Identity, Mission, Accountability, Discipleship

Teaching: This particular communal response highlights the community accountability aspect of this teaching. As followers of Jesus, we have the unique responsibility (Galatians 6:1-10) of helping each other be consistent in rejecting sin and embracing the way of Jesus.

Activity/Response: Students will each take a card (or even two or three, if available) and write the name of a Christian friend, giving that friend permission to speak into their lives at any time about their relationships with Jesus. As students make this decision, they can take time to really consider what speaking the truth in love means when they help another follower of Jesus (Ephesians 4:2-16).

Supplies:
- Tables and tapestries or tablecloths (optional)
- Permission cards printed out on 8.5 x 11 paper and then cut
- Pens (as needed, either on the tables or under every seat)

Signs/Directions: On accompanying CD

LOVE AND MARRIAGE

2 Prayer Stations

Teaching (general): In Hebrew culture at the time of Jesus, the people acted according to the moral law (passed down from Moses through the Hebrew Scriptures) and religious obligation. We, too, in our cultural context, have a tendency to act according to what's "normal" and "expected." Whenever Jesus talks about relationships—be it a relationship with God or with other human beings—he consistently surprises us. People are far more important to God (and must be to us as followers of Jesus!) than we could have guessed. We have to take Jesus seriously when he teaches us how to value people in our lives.

After the Teaching: Adequate time is given (with live or recorded music playing) for students to interact with this Prayer Station according to what was just taught. It's always important to walk through the instructions thoroughly, helping the students see the symbolism and the prayer focus that tie into the teaching.

These Prayer Stations encourage students to be honest about areas of conflict in relationships—and to humbly and immediately communicate with those they're in conflict with.

Love and Marriage: Praying about Relationships

Scripture: Matthew 5:31-32

Themes: Sexuality, Love, Communication, Honesty, Peace

Purpose: It directly ties into Jesus' Sermon on the Mount teaching from Matthew 5:31-32 on the topic of love and marriage—and on the weight of loyalty and fidelity in relationships.

Teaching: Sexuality is a huge part of our identity as humans. And how we live out our sexuality is very important to Jesus. No surprise—many of Jesus' teachings put emphasis on our private lives and hidden motives/attitudes of the heart. Jesus invites us to follow him in valuing sexuality and relationships in a completely new way as members of the kingdom of heaven.

Activity/Response: As students approach the Prayer Station, instructions (see sign text on accompanying CD) are given to students to read, as well as the corresponding Scripture passage. More than one student can participate at this station at a time.

With all the photos on the table, students will be able to reflect about love, marriage, and singleness in general—afterward praying for those in their lives who are in those levels of relationship. This station can incorporate photography from artists in your church community or found elsewhere (on photo subscription sites online, stock photography, magazines/newspapers, etc.).

Supplies:
- Table and tablecloth or tapestries
- Instructional signs on 8.5 x 11 paper
- 2 or 3 candles
- Black construction paper (as needed) to paste on backs of photos as matting
- Glue or Scotch tape
- 15 to 20 relationship photographs (couples, singles, conflict in relationships, etc.)
- Tabletop easels or other display aids (optional)

Setting Up the Station: Place a tablecloth on the table—and put the instructional signs and Scripture passage in multiple places where they can be easily read. Paste or tape the photos on black construction paper as "matting." Arrange the photo assortment accessibly for the students to look through and pick up if desired.

Signs/Directions: On accompanying CD

Love and Marriage: Building Up the Family

Scripture: Matthew 5:31-32; 7:24-27

Themes: Family, Sexuality, Love, Communication, Honesty, Peace

Purpose: It directly ties into Jesus' Sermon on the Mount teaching from Matthew 5:31-32 on the topic of love and marriage (as well as Matthew 7:24-27 on the weight of commitment and family development).

Teaching: Family is a community of lives intertwined. Jesus talks about the people of God as family—children of God the Father. The family unit is a beautiful human illustration of God's way of relationships and communication. We must follow the teachings of Jesus and not our culture when it comes to thinking about family.

Activity/Response: As students approach the Prayer Station/table, instructions (see sign text on accompanying CD) are given to students to read, as well as the corresponding Scripture passage. More than one student can participate at this station at a time.

With the centralized basket of miscellaneous Legos, the students can build a house. This act will aid them in praying for the building up of their families and the families they know.

Supplies:
- Table and tablecloth or tapestries
- Instructional signs on 8.5 x 11 paper
- 2 or 3 candles
- Basket or decorated box
- Large assortment of Legos

Setting Up the Station: Place a tablecloth on the table—and put the instructional signs and Scripture passage in multiple places where they can be easily read. Place the Lego assortment centrally and make sure it's accessible. Provide plenty of space so students can construct their houses.

Signs/Directions: On accompanying CD

BEING THE SALT OF THE EARTH

2 Prayer Stations

Themes: Sharing Jesus with Others, Evangelism, Integrity

Purpose: These two prayer stations directly tie into Jesus' Sermon on the Mount teaching from Matthew 5:13 about being "salt" of the earth.

Teaching: In New Testament times, salt was used as a preservative (since they had no ice), as well as for flavor. Jesus uses salt as a metaphor here to tell those who follow him that they should be the "flavor" of him (and the kingdom of God) to those they come in contact with, as well as preserve God's goodness for those around them.

After the Teaching: After the teaching, time is given (with live or recorded music) for students to interact with the Prayer Stations that directly tie into what was just taught. It's always important to walk through the instructions well, helping the students see the symbolism and the prayer focus that tie into the teaching.

These Prayer Stations are about praying for others around the world and remembering the global church.

Being the Salt of the Earth: Pretzels

Activity/Response: As students approach the Prayer Station, the first things they see are the Scripture passages that were just taught about being salt. The dominant "You Are the Salt of the Earth" message are the words they see on the table itself. Instructions (see sign text on accompanying CD) are given to students to read, as well as the corresponding Scripture passage. More than one student can participate at this station at a time.

Students then eat both the salted and unsalted pretzels; as they do, they're asked to notice the difference between them—as well as how salty food causes hunger for more food! They're then asked to determine how salty they are for the world around them—have they lost their saltiness that increases others' hunger for the hope that's in them? Finally they're given time at the Prayer Station to pray that Jesus would increase their saltiness if they've lost some of his "flavor" in their spirits.

Supplies:
- Table and tablecloth
- Instructional signs on 8.5 x 11 paper
- Bag of salted pretzels
- Bag of unsalted pretzels
- Two bowls for the pretzels
- Butcher paper and paint or markers to paint "You Are the Salt of the Earth" and "If the Salt Loses Its Saltiness…"
- Large salt shaker and small shaker
- Small decorative signs labeled "Salted" and "Unsalted"
- Small pieces of decorative construction paper with the Matthew 5:13 passage on it for placement on the table (or just the passage itself on table)
- 2 or 3 small candles

Setting Up the Station: On the table with tablecloth, place two bowls and fill one with salted pretzels and the other with unsalted pretzels. Set up the signs in front of each bowl so it's clear which one is salted and which one isn't. Place the salt shakers where appropriate. Hang the "If the Salt Loses Its Saltiness…" sign behind the table and place directly on the table the sign that says "You Are the Salt of the Earth" as the prominent element. Place on the table the instructions for the Prayer Station (included on the CD is a sample sign that can be reproduced) in between the bowls or on each side of the bowls.

Signs/Directions: On accompanying CD

Being the Salt of the Earth: Map Salting

Activity/Response: As students approach the Prayer Station, the first things they see are the Scripture passages that were just taught about being salt. The dominant "We Are the Salt of the Earth" message is the phrase they see on the table itself. Instructions (see sign text on accompanying CD) are given to students to read, as well as the corresponding Scripture passage. More than one student can participate at this station at a time.

Students are then instructed to pick up some salt crystals and drop them or place them on a specific country on the global map lying on the table, praying as they do for the Christians in those countries to be salt to those around them. The students also are encouraged to pray for the countries they've placed salt upon.

Supplies:
- Table and tablecloth or tapestries
- Instructional signs on 8.5 x 11 paper
- 1 or 2 bowls
- Salt crystals or regular salt in the bowls
- World map
- Butcher paper and paint or markers to paint "We Are the Salt of the Earth"
- Decorative construction paper with the entire Scripture passage printed on it and placed around the station
- 2 or 3 small candles

Setting Up the Station: On the table with the tablecloth or on the floor with tapestries, place a world map. Behind the Prayer Station in a visible place, hang or place the sign that says "We Are the Salt of the Earth." Place on the table or near the map a bowl containing salt crystals (or regular salt can be used). If this is on the ground, place pillows all around it so students can kneel as they pray. Place the instructions around the map so students can clearly read what to do. Place small, decorative copies of Matthew 5:13 around the map.

Signs/Directions: On accompanying CD

THE DOOR

2 Communal Art Expressions; 2 Prayer Stations

The Door: The Afterlife & Eternity

Scripture: Matthew 7:13-29, along with other passages that address eternity and the afterlife (e.g., Matthew 24, 25)

Themes: The Afterlife, Eternity, Salvation, Repentance, Relationships

Purpose: It directly ties into Jesus' Sermon on the Mount teaching from Matthew 7 about eternity and the afterlife.

Option: It may be most advantageous to teach this two-faceted topic of heaven and hell over the course of two weeks. An additional third week may be most helpful to allow time for prayer, Communion, and reflection. This Communal Art Expression has the most impact if used in three parts.

Teaching: Jesus didn't hesitate to answer his followers' spoken and unspoken questions about the afterlife and eternity. He used multiple metaphors to teach that eternity, in many ways, is an extension of this life's choices. The kingdom of God is eternal. Once again, he challenges his followers with the difficulty of eternal choices. There are many views in our culture about eternity—just as there were in Jesus' day (the perspectives of the Pharisees versus the Sadducees, for example). Jesus says he is the way to being with God eternally, and in following his teachings, we can live in the kingdom of God on earth—heaven future and heaven now.

This teaching focus presents a great opportunity to clearly and concisely present a few of these truths to students—helping them understand theological scholarship and how mystery is always present as we study about God and try to grasp a corner of who God is and how God works. However, as this topic can bring up cultural stereotypes regarding heaven and hell, it may be helpful to address the stereotypes, comparing and contrasting them with some of the sketches Scripture gives.

During the Teaching on Heaven: One or two artists paint on a giant canvas centrally located. They may want to use peaceful colors and perhaps go for a tranquil landscape. This is to be a visual illustration of heaven as a place of ultimate peace and wholeness in relationship with God and each other.

During the Teaching on Hell: One or two artists (either the same or different artists from the week previous) take the same giant canvas, centrally located, upon which the heaven scene was painted. Throughout the teaching, they can blacken the scene with WASHABLE paint. (It's KEY to have washable paint in order to carry out the final piece of this Communal Art Expression the following week.) This is a visual illustration of hell being a place without relationship with God and people, without beauty, peace, or rest—just complete blackness.

After the Teaching (or at an additional gathering): A facilitator can share Scripture passages (e.g., Hebrews 10:19-25) that describe the hope of a relationship with Jesus now *and* the hope of heaven in the future. After the teaching, time is given (with live or recorded music) for students to interact with this Communal Art Expression.

Activity/Response: The giant, now-blackened canvas should be centrally located in the room with plenty of space around it so students can easily interact with it. You may wish to place Scripture passages around it on the theme of Heaven Future / Heaven Now for students to reflect on as they engage in the Communal Art Expression.

Students will take cloths or sponges, and with the water provided, literally scrub away the washable grey/black paint that marred the beautiful scene underneath it. As they scrub away the blackness, they can thank God for reversing the curse of sin and death in this world and in eternity so we can look forward to heaven.

Supplies:
Weeks 1 and 2:
- Drop cloth under the painting
- Giant blank canvas
- Paints and supplies for the artists
- Additional lighting for the artists if needed (perhaps even clip-on desk lamps that you can attach to the wall, a chair, or an easel)

Week 3:
- 5-15 sponges and cloths
- Buckets of soapy, warm water
- Butcher paper or construction paper with paint or markers for each Scripture passage
- Adequate lighting around the painting area (house lights, clip-on desk lamps that you can attach to the wall or another surface, floor lamps, candelabras, etc.)

Setting Up the Station: *Weeks 1 & 2 only:* Set up the artists in a visible location during the teaching. Place instructional signs and Scripture passages in multiple places where they can be easily read. *Week 3:* Provide plenty of sponges and cloths in buckets of warm, soapy water. Put a thick drop cloth underneath the communal art area, since the paint will be heavily diluted when students sponge it off and water will get everywhere.

Sign/Directions: On accompanying CD

The Door: Two Roads

Scripture: Matthew 7:13-14

Themes: The Afterlife, Eternity, Salvation, Repentance, Relationships

Purpose: It directly ties into Jesus' Sermon on the Mount teaching from Matthew 7 about eternity and the afterlife.

Teaching: Jesus didn't hesitate to answer his followers' spoken and unspoken questions about the afterlife and eternity. He used multiple metaphors to teach that eternity, in many ways, is an extension of this life's choices. The kingdom of God is eternal. Once again, he challenges his followers with the difficulty of eternal choices. There are many views in our culture about eternity—just as there were in Jesus' day (the perspectives of the Pharisees versus the Sadducees, for example). Jesus says he is the way to being with God eternally, and in following his teachings, we can live in the kingdom of God on earth—heaven future and heaven now.

This teaching focus presents a great opportunity to clearly and concisely present a few of these truths to students—helping them understand theological scholarship and how mystery is always present as we study about God and try to grasp a corner of who God is and how God works.

During the Teaching: You may want to have both a gate and a door (or two doors or two gates) as visuals for the students during the message, with large and legible signs reading "The Narrow Gate (or Door)" and "The Wide Gate (or "Door"), depending on which visuals you choose.

After the Teaching: After the teaching, time is given (with live or recorded music) for students to interact with the Prayer Stations that directly tie into what was just taught. It's always important to walk through the instructions well, helping the students see the symbolism and the prayer focus that tie into the teaching.

Activity/Response: As students approach the Prayer Station, instructions (see sign text on accompanying CD) are given to students to read, as well as the corresponding Scripture passage. More than one student can participate at this station at a time.

Immediately the students should see two different roads with a lot of pins stuck in the wide road—symbolic of the majority of people's life paths without relationship with Jesus. As students think of individuals in their lives who're walking on the wide road, they are to prayerfully move pins to the narrow road. This symbolic and visual act will encourage students to pray that their friends and family members will enter into relationships with Jesus and walk through life in a new way.

Supplies:
- Table and tablecloth or tapestries
- Instructional signs on 8.5 x 11 paper
- 2 or 3 candles
- Large bulletin board (on which to place the two "roads")
- Butcher paper or colored paper with which to create a wide and a narrow road on the bulletin board
- Multicolored pushpins

Setting Up the Station: Place a tablecloth on the table—and put the instructional signs and Scripture passage in multiple places where they can be easily read. Cut the butcher paper to size and tape it to the bulletin board in the shape of two roads. Stick the pins in the wide road as well as a couple on the narrow road to give the students an idea of what they'll be doing.

Signs/Directions: On accompanying CD

The Door: Building Our House

Scripture: Matthew 7:24-29; 16:18-19

Themes: Attitudes of the Heart, Authenticity, Discipline, Obedience

Purpose: It directly ties into Jesus' Sermon on the Mount teaching from Matthew 7:24-29, as well as Matthew 16:18-19.

Teaching: Jesus uses the rich imagery of construction to illustrate that with every step in his way of life, another nail is being hammered in a life constructed on firm rock—and no storm, no matter how furious, can devastate it. This passage is illuminated further, diving into the symbolism of bad weather—unexpected or progressively arriving life circumstances, emotions (one's own or others'), etc. The gods of the nations around Israel historically used weather to communicate wrath or blessing to people who survived on the growth of agriculture and livestock. Jesus is here emphasizing the trustworthiness of his way of life as standing up to all other religions and lifestyles.

Matthew 16:18-19 ties in perfectly here, as it describes when Jesus first uttered the word *church*—when he was physically standing in a place in Israel called "The Gates of Hades," which was thought to be the entrance to hell itself and where many gods were worshiped in niches in the rocks. At this important spiritual location, Jesus notes that his church will be built on rock (the same metaphor used in Matthew 7:24-29) and nothing can keep it from standing interminably.

During the Teaching: Centrally place the previously constructed house as a visual representation of what's being taught. You may want to place it in front of a panel or cross to enhance the visual as being a spiritual house.

After the Teaching: A facilitator shares other Scripture passages (e.g., 1 Peter 2:5) that talk about our lives being built like a house—individually and collectively as the church of Jesus. After detailed instructions are clearly explained, time is given (with live or recorded music) for students to interact with this Communal Art Expression.

Activity/Response: The facilitator explains that as the music is playing, everyone in the room can hammer a nail into the house, symbolic of choosing to build their lives with the teachings of Jesus—being his church. It can be shared that even the sound of the nails being hammered during this time of worship is a powerful symbol that we aren't just worshiping with our words, but will be choosing daily to build our lives in Jesus.

As the facilitator is sharing, two previously prepared monitors should move to the house with hammers in hand. They are the "damage control" individuals who hand the hammer and nail to the individuals and motion where they can hammer their nail.

Students approach the Prayer Station, and as they're waiting in line, they can read the Scripture passage(s) posted around the space (see accompanying CD). Have several displays so many students can reflect as they wait. When the students approach the communal art monitors, the monitors hand students both a hammer and a nail, motioning where to place the nail. Only minor amendments to the construction should happen. Perhaps the structure will only need a roof and walls.

Supplies:
- Wood, nails, and tools to construct a dog house-sized house (ask a construction-inclined member of your church community to help out with this!)
- 2 to 4 hammers
- Long nails (one for every student)
- Sheet or drop cloth to place under the house
- Butcher paper or construction paper with paint or markers for each Scripture passage
- Adequate lighting around the house area (house lights, clip-on desk lamps that you can attach to the wall or another surface, floor lamps, candelabras, etc.)

Setting Up the Station: Put the sheet or drop cloth down, then the previously constructed house on top of it, in a central location in the room. (Note: Allow plenty of room around the house so many students can visit the house at once after the teaching.) Tape, paste, or lay the Scripture passages around the area with whatever lighting you'll need.

Signs/Directions: On accompanying CD

The Door: Heaven Later / Heaven Now

Scripture: Matthew 7:13-14, along with other passages that address eternity and the afterlife

Themes: The Afterlife, Eternity, Salvation, Repentance, Relationships

Purpose: It directly ties into Jesus' Sermon on the Mount teaching from Matthew 7 about eternity and the afterlife.

Teaching: Jesus didn't hesitate to answer his followers' spoken and unspoken questions about the afterlife and eternity. He used multiple metaphors to teach that eternity, in many ways, is an extension of this life's choices. The kingdom of God is eternal. Once again, he challenges his followers with the difficulty of eternal choices. There are many views in our culture about eternity—just as there were in Jesus' day (the perspectives of the Pharisees versus the Sadducees, for example). Jesus says that he is the way to being with God eternally, and in following his teachings, we can live in the kingdom of God on earth—heaven future and heaven now.

This teaching focus presents a great opportunity to clearly and concisely present a few of these truths to students—helping them understand theological scholarship and how mystery is always present as we study about God and try to grasp a corner of who God is and how God works.

After the Teaching: Time is given (with live or recorded music) for students to interact with the Prayer Stations that directly tie into what was just taught. It's always important to walk through the instructions well, helping the students see the symbolism and the prayer focus that tie into the teaching.

Activity/Response: As students approach the Prayer Station, instructions (see sign text on accompanying CD) are given to students to read, as well as the corresponding Scripture passage. More than one student can participate at this station at a time.

Students will have space to read and reflect on Scripture passages about the hope of Heaven Future and the reality of having a corner of Heaven Now—taking this life seriously. They can take the time to write a prayer of thanksgiving or a prayer of life dedication on one of the sides of the butcher paper offered.

Supplies:

- Table and tablecloth or tapestries
- Instructional signs and Scripture passages on 8.5 x 11 paper
- Large sheet(s) of butcher paper
- 4 to 8 pens

Setting Up the Station: Place a tablecloth on the table—and put the instructional signs in multiple places where they can be easily read. Cut the butcher paper in two pieces on each side of the table. Label one side "Heaven Future" and the other side "Heaven Now." Place the corresponding Scripture passages around the labeled butcher paper. Place pens centrally.

Signs/Directions: On accompanying CD

TRANSFORMATION

4 Prayer Stations;
1 Communal Art Expression

Purpose: These Prayer Stations and Communal Art Expression fit well during New Year's or the beginning of a school year when students are thinking about life change and personal resolutions.

Teaching (general): Every New Year's Day or the first day of a new school year brings hope of change. We may have a desire to work on sin issues we're dealing with, to shed poor habits or develop new habits, to meet someone, or find a new job. No matter what our desires or resolutions may be, we have great hope the new beginning will bring about something better. However, when we feel down about ourselves or discouraged, we wonder if change is possible. This is a great opportunity to discuss the issue of spiritual identity with practical application points to help us engage in the changing work God desires for us.

After the Teaching: Time is given (with live or recorded music) for students to interact with these Prayer Stations and Communal Art Expression according to what was just taught. It's always important to walk through the instructions well, helping the students see the symbolism and the prayer focus that tie into the teaching.

Transformation: Laying Down Our Fears

Scripture: Matthew 9:2-8; Mark 2:1-12; Romans 12:1-2

Themes: Change, Surrender, Fear, Hope

Teaching: This particular Prayer Station focuses on a conversation between Jesus and a paralyzed man and the man's friends. This story helps us address some reasons why the thought of changing can paralyze us. Whether it's our anxiety about being alone, fears of the future, past regrets, or doubts of our abilities, God has given us community (the paralyzed man's friends), himself (Jesus immediately said, "Be encouraged"), and freedom from guilt (Jesus forgave the man) to enable seemingly impossible change (only Jesus was the source of change for the man).

Activity/Response: As students approach the Prayer Station, instructions (see sign text on accompanying CD) are given to students to read, as well as the corresponding Scripture passage. More than one student can participate at this station at a time.

Students will literally lie down on the mats—just like the blind man in the story. They will write down their fears about change and ask Jesus to replace those fears with his love and peace and strength for change. They will keep that list in their Bibles through the next week to continue praying and giving over all to Jesus.

Supplies:
- Tapestries and drapery to decorate a simple chair
- 4 to 8 beach mats (straw mats from drug stores around summer time)
- Instructional signs on 8.5 x 11 paper
- Candles or soft floor lighting
- Pillows as needed
- 3 x 5 index cards or square sheets of paper
- 4 to 8 pens

Setting Up the Station: Roll out three or four mats on the floor and put the rest of the beach mats in a basket or box for students to take as needed. Place the pens and papers around each mat for the students to easily grab. Put the instructional signs and Scripture passage in multiple places where they can be easily read. Lay pillows on the floor for students to use as they kneel or lay on the mats in prayer.

Signs/Directions: On accompanying CD

Transformation: Mirrors

Scripture: Luke 12:6-7; 19:1-9; Ephesians 2:10; Psalm 27:10

Themes: Change, Surrender, Fear, Hope, Identity, Insecurities

Teaching: This particular Prayer Station focuses on students' identity and self-esteem issues. This teaching can focus on the life of Zacchaeus, who was seen as a sinner and lowly by others due to his vocation; he also was short, which must have impacted him in that culture, and his wealth was not meeting his spiritual needs. When Zacchaeus met Jesus, his life was transformed. In Ephesians 2:10, we read that we're each created as God's "workmanship." The word *workmanship* not only means unique, special, and beautiful, but also our modern words *poetry* and *poem* are derived from it.

We often judge our worth by appearance (How do I look?), achievement (What have I accomplished?), approval (How well am I liked?), or affluence (What do I own?). However, we find that Jesus—no matter how insignificant we feel, what others say, or what we do—loves, affirms, and wants us.

Activity/Response: As students approach the Prayer Station, instructions (see sign text on accompanying CD) are given to students to read, as well as the corresponding Scripture passage. More than one student can participate at this station at a time.

Students will approach Mirror 1, which has on it the questions, *How do I look? What have I accomplished? How well am I liked? What do I own?* Students will have the opportunity to ask themselves how they measure their worth. They then move to Mirror 2 and reflect on their identities as God's beautiful, unique poems—works of art. They can take a Scripture card with them to remember what God says about their identities.

Supplies:
- Table with tablecloth or tapestries
- Instructional signs on 8.5 x 11 paper
- 2 or 3 candles and clip lighting as needed (for the mirrors)
- Markers or paint to print or paint the signs for each mirror

- 2 large mirrors (borrow from a member of your church community!)
- Create a Scripture card (wallet-size) with key passages about our identity in Jesus for students to take with them (optional)

Setting Up the Station: Put the instructional signs and Scripture passage in multiple places on the table—with candles for lighting and decoration—where they can be easily read. Place the Scripture cards on the table in a box or basket for students to take with them. Put the mirrors beside each other with clear numbers pasted on them—as well as the signs.

Signs/Directions: On accompanying CD

Transformation: Life Patterns

Scripture: Psalm 119:9-11; Romans 7:15-25; 2 Corinthians 10:15; James 1:14-15; 5:16

Themes: Change, Surrender, Fear, Hope, Identity, Insecurities, Habits, Temptations

Teaching: This Prayer Station addresses the persistent habits and temptations that plague us. In order to live out our God-created identities as God's workmanship, we must break out of the ruts we're in. Some ruts are obvious—promiscuity and pornography, for example. However, some habits easily slip under our radar and are just as toxic to us and those around us. For example: Gossip, poor eating, lying, watching too much TV, spending too much time wrapped up online, or being selfish with our time in general. This is a great opportunity to bring up some very clear and practical examples of what to do when we want to break out of a bad habit and avoid temptations. Have students ask:

- When am I most tempted?
- Where am I most tempted?
- Who is with me when I'm most tempted?
- What temporary benefits do I get when I give in?

Activity/Response: As students approach the Prayer Station, instructions (see sign text on accompanying CD) are given to students to read, as well as the corresponding Scripture passage. More than one student can participate at this station at a time.

Students will use stencils, sponges, and paint to create a pattern on a sheet of paper. They'll have the opportunity to think about their life patterns. If there's a pattern they need to break, they can take scissors to cut the paper pattern they've created. If they have some positive habits in their lives, they can look at the paper pattern, asking God for consistency.

Supplies:
- Table with tablecloth or tapestries
- Instructional signs on 8.5 x 11 paper
- 2 or 3 candles
- Finger or tempera paint
- 5 x 6 sheets of paper (one for each student)
- Miscellaneous stencils and sponges cut in various shapes and in different sizes
- Little cups or dishes for the paint

- 4 to 6 paintbrushes to help with application
- Water in bowls to help keep the paint wet
- 4 to 6 pairs of scissors

Setting Up the Station: Put the instructional signs and Scripture passage in multiple places on the table—with candles for lighting and decoration—where they can be easily read. Spread stencils, paints, brushes, scissors, and paper on the table for easy access. Light the table with a few candles.

Signs/Directions: On accompanying CD

Transformation: Gaining Spiritual Strength

Scripture: Romans 12:1-2; 1 Corinthians 9:24-27; 1 Timothy 4:7

Themes: Change, Surrender, Fear, Hope, Identity, Insecurities, Habits, Temptations, Spiritual Discipline

Teaching: This Prayer Station addresses the difference between "trying" and "training" when it comes to change. It's the Spirit of God who changes us—but we can align ourselves with God in discipline to allow change to happen. Too often we're discouraged by failure, wishing there were a formula for instant change. God does instigate dramatic and immediate change at times, but most often, God instigates a process over time. If one attempts to lift a 200-pound barbell in a gym with no training, one is unlikely to realize success. However, if you train over time, you can get to the point where you can lift 200 pounds.

In the Gospel accounts of the life of Jesus, as well as in the other New Testament books, we constantly see patterns of people who fasted, prayed, knew the Scriptures deeply, served with their gifts in the church, etc. The goal of these spiritual disciplines is to have us change into more-worshiping lovers of God and other people (Matthew 22:37-39)—not so we feel as though we're achieving some status with God or simply doing our duty. The goal is to see the fruit of the Spirit in our lives (Galatians 5:22-23). Just as doctors give physicals and an auto mechanic checks a car to see how the primary gauges are running, we too must take inventory of our spiritual lives and help each other develop spiritual disciplines as God's church.

Activity/Response: As students approach the Prayer Station, instructions (see sign text on accompanying CD) are given to students to read, as well as the corresponding Scripture passage. More than one student can participate at this station at a time.

Students can lift some hand weights or use a portable abdominal exercise machine as they think about how physical training challenges and develops our physical strength. They can take the time to ask themselves in what areas they need spiritual training for challenge and strength. Space will be available around the station for them to pray and ask God for spiritual discipline in practical, everyday moments in their lives.

Supplies:

- Table with tablecloth or tapestries
- Instructional signs on 8.5 x 11 paper
- 2 or 3 candles
- Light hand weights or a bench if possible
- Miscellaneous work-out items (a ball, jump rope, etc.)
- Tapestries or a rug for students to lie on as they use the equipment

Setting Up the Station: Put the instructional signs and Scripture passage in multiple places where they can be easily read. Arrange the workout equipment in several areas for easy use by multiple students. Light the table with a few candles.

Signs/Directions: On accompanying CD

Transformation: Apple & Honey

Scripture: Matthew 9:2-8; Mark 2:1-12; Romans 12:1-2; Lamentations 3:21-24

Themes: Change, Surrender, Fear, Hope

Teaching: This particular Communal Art Expression highlights a tradition of the Jewish New Year (Rosh Hashanah) celebrated in September (first and second days of Tishri on the Jewish calendar). It's a time when Jewish people stop and reflect on their lives and ask forgiveness from God before moving ahead into the next year. They blow the *shofar* (a horn) when this happens, as well as eat apples dipped in honey as a symbol of their hope of a sweet New Year. We can observe this Jewish custom as we direct our hopes and fears to our God.

Activity/Response: As students approach the Prayer Station, instructions (see sign text on accompanying CD) are given to students to read, as well as the corresponding Scripture passage. Provide 10 to 20 stations for students to use, depending on your group size. At every station, there should be a bowl with apples and a bowl with honey. As they dip the apple in the honey, they can take the time to give their hopes to God, asking him to make this New Year sweet.

Supplies:
- Tables and tapestries or tablecloths
- Instructional signs and Scripture passages on 8.5 x 11 paper
- Candle for every station (for lighting purposes as well as ambiance)
- 2 bowls for every station
- Apples, as needed (Note: Since apples turn brown quickly, you may need to slice them during the message portion of the gathering so they're fresh for this Communal Art Expression)
- Honey, as needed

Setting Up the Station: Decorate the tables with tapestries. At every station, place a candle, a bowl with honey, and a bowl with apple slices, along with the instructional signs and the Scripture passage.

Signs/Directions: On accompanying CD

WHOLLY YOURS

1 Communal Art Expression; 2 Prayer Stations

Purpose: This Communal Art Expression and two Prayer Stations directly tie into the topic of holistic life stewardship that can be a series over a few weeks, possibly at the beginning of a new year.

Teaching: We love our possessions just as much as we love our accomplishments and abilities. We can become ashamed or feel sorry for ourselves when we compare our riches with those of our friends or neighbors who seemingly have more than we do. We boast about and are protective of what we own and are automatically defensive about what we don't own. The law of diminishing returns is illustrated in our lives every time we get caught up in greedily wanting the next best thing in technology or fashion. Everything we watch, read, or talk about reinforces this way of being in the world.

Scripture teaches us a different way of living and thinking about what we own. It tells us even our bodies are given to us by God. Everything actually belongs to our Creator, who's given us this life as a gift—our bodies, time, money, relationships, family, work, skills, abilities… *everything*. We're accountable to God for what he's entrusted us with (Matthew 25:14-29; 2 Corinthians 5:10). Therefore we should have attitudes of joy and gratitude as we healthily manage our lives with his wisdom and strength.

After the Teaching: Time is given (with live or recorded music) for students to interact with the Communal Art Expression or Prayer Stations that directly tie into what was just taught. It's always important to walk through the instructions well, helping the students see the symbolism and the prayer focus that tie into the teaching.

COMMUNAL ART EXPRESSION

Wholly Yours: Holistic Life Dedication

Scripture: Psalm 24:1; 139; Proverbs 11:24; Ecclesiastes 3; Matthew 6:21-24; 25:14-29; Luke 16:10-15; 2 Corinthians 5:10; 9:6-7; Colossians 1:16; and other passages about stewardship

Themes: Stewardship, Identity, Surrender, Money, Purpose

Activity/Response: Students will bring money with them to the communal art space to place in the basket as an act of worship and sacrifice. They can then write prayers of holistic life dedication to God, placing them in the basket. Incense is burning as a symbol of prayers rising to God.

When explaining the essence of a holistic life dedication prayer, make sure students understand that it's about committing everything to God—finances, you love life, your friendships, your family, your job, your school, your belongings. *Everything*.

Supplies:
- Table and tablecloth or tapestries
- Incense (be careful because some people are sensitive to smells and/or have allergies) and 2 or 3 incense holders
- 2 or 3 candles
- 1 to 3 baskets
- Blank 3 x 5 cards or squares of paper
- 8 to 10 pens

Setting Up the Station: Place a tablecloth on the table—and put the Scripture passages in multiple places where they can be easily read. Light the incense as a symbol and place it centrally. Put paper and pens near the baskets.

Signs/Directions: Scripture on accompanying CD; no directional signs needed (verbal instructions should be sufficient).

Wholly Yours: Time

Scripture: Psalm 24:1; 139; Ecclesiastes 3; Matthew 25:14-29; 1 Corinthians 6:19-20; 2 Corinthians 5:10; Colossians 1:16; and other passages about time and stewardship

Themes: Stewardship, Identity, Surrender, Time, Purpose

Activity/Response: As students approach the Prayer Station, instructions (see sign text on accompanying CD) are given to students to read, as well as the corresponding Scripture passage. More than one student can participate at this station at a time.

Students will take time looking at all the clocks and their labels, which symbolize how all time is used. They'll ask themselves how they spend their time and what activities they should spend more or less time on. They can use the space to give all their hours to God—asking him to help them be wise with their time.

Supplies:
- Table and tablecloth or tapestries
- Assorted photos of clocks
- Alarm clocks, house clocks, etc.
- Pens, markers, or paints to create clock labels (example labels: TV, internet, talking on the phone, friends, family, church meetings, hobbies, shopping, alone time, reading)

Setting Up the Station: Place a tablecloth on the table—and put the instructional signs and Scripture passages in multiple places where they can be easily read. Label every clock or clock photo.

Signs/Directions: On accompanying CD

Wholly Yours: Money

Scripture: Psalm 24:1; Proverbs 11:24; Matthew 6:21-24; Luke 16:10-15; 2 Corinthians 9:6-7; and other passages about money and stewardship

Themes: Stewardship, Identity, Surrender, Money, Purpose

Teaching: Money is such an important subject for us to address as followers of Jesus. It's used countless times in the Bible in narratives and parables about attitudes of the heart. Every spending decision we make is actually a spiritual decision—revealing where our heart's priorities are.

Activity/Response: As students approach the Prayer Station, instructions (see sign text on accompanying CD) are given to students to read, as well as the corresponding Scripture passages. More than one student can participate at this station at a time.

Students will take time looking at the penny graphs and statistics of how money is typically spent in our nation or in your specific county. They'll ask themselves how they spend their money and what items they should spend more or less money on. They can use the space to give all their money to God—asking him to help them be wise with their finances and generous when it comes to others' needs.

Supplies:
- Table and tablecloth or tapestries
- Tons of pennies (even fake coins if necessary)
- Statistics (from online or a resource book) of how much money is spent on what in America or their county

Setting Up the Station: Place a tablecloth on the table—and put the instructional signs and Scripture passages in multiple places where they can be easily read. Create rough three-dimensional bar graphs with labels for each stack of coins—saying the specific amount that most people spend on that particular area of life (e.g., food, music, games, entertainment in general).

Signs/Directions: On accompanying CD

3 Additional
Prayer Stations

Parables: Lost Sheep

Scripture: Luke 15:4-10; John 10:7-18; and other passages about sheep and God as Shepherd

Themes: Pride, Love, Humility, Compassion, Discrimination

Purpose: It directly corresponds to Jesus' parable of the lost sheep from Luke 15:4-10.

Teaching: Like the rabbis of his time, Jesus used simple word-pictures, called parables, to help people understand who God is and how God's kingdom (or reign) operates. Like a skillful artist, Jesus painted evocative pictures with characters taken from everyday life to create miniature plays or dramas to illustrate his messages. His stories appealed to young and old, poor and rich, and learned and unlearned. This was Jesus' most common way of teaching. These word-pictures challenged the heart and imagination to respond to God's love and truth. Jesus used the ordinary in his parables to point to another order of reality—hidden, yet visible to those who had "eyes to see" and "ears to hear." His parables are still like buried treasure waiting to be discovered (Matthew 13:44).

This parable of the lost sheep is followed by two other parables addressing the loss of something valuable that's pursued with great earnest. Jesus uses this repetition to underscore the importance of the parables' message.

Shepherding was one of the principal vocations of Jesus' day. Shepherds, although important to society, were often looked down upon as a part of the lowest class of society because of their often-unkempt appearance and their livestock-dedicated lifestyles. Jesus often refers to God or himself (John 10:7-18) as the Good Shepherd and to those who follow him as sheep—whom Jesus leads, tends, and pursues when lost.

The lost sheep in this parable are those that belong to Jesus (i.e., have chosen to believe and follow Jesus) but have wandered off and are outside the flock (i.e., the community of faith). Perhaps these lost sheep haven't realized how far they've wandered or aren't even aware they've trekked away. Jesus emphasizes his commitment to these followers of his and the great lengths he'll go to in order to bring them back into relationship with God and his followers.

We, as followers of Jesus, can join him in his pursuit of lost sheep in our lives through prayer and consistent companionship—no matter what the cost or challenge.

After the Teaching: Adequate time is given (with live or recorded music playing) for students to interact with this Prayer Station according to what was just taught. It's always important to walk through the instructions thoroughly, helping the students see the symbolism and the prayer focus that tie into the teaching.

Activity/Response: Students will write the first names of Christian friends who've wandered off or rejected their beliefs or the way of Jesus. (They may need to write "me" on the cards if they believe they've wandered away as well.) Then they bring the cards to the designated stations, praying that their friends will sense Jesus pursuing them and that God would bring people into their lives to remind them who they are as followers of Jesus.

Supplies:
- 1 or 2 tables and tablecloths or tapestries
- 2 to 6 candles
- Painting of Jesus, his eyes, a shepherd's crook or rod, photos (or art) of sheep
- 1 or 2 two boxes or baskets
- Blank 3 x 5 cards or squares of paper (as needed)
- Pens or pencils (as needed) for either under the seats or at the station(s)

Setting Up the Stations: Set up two stations in difference places in the room for traffic purposes or one large station if suitable for your group size. Decorate the tables with tapestries and candles. Place a shepherd/sheep art piece or symbol (rod, staff; painting of Jesus, his eyes, etc.) centrally with a box or basket nearby where students can place their cards.

Either hand out the cards to students when they enter the gathering, during the gathering at some point, or place the cards on the actual stations.

Signs/Directions: On accompanying CD

Sticky-Note Relationships: Resolving Conflict

Scripture: Matthew 5:21-26

Themes: Conflict in Relationships, Honesty, Forgiveness, Humility

Purpose: It directly ties into Jesus' Sermon on the Mount teaching from Matthew 5:21-26 about the importance of dealing with conflict in relationships.

Teaching: Jesus shocks his followers with this teaching, comparing attitudes of anger with the act of murder! The teaching is given on the importance of dealing with conflict *immediately* because it's such a huge issue of the heart. It's not only important to honestly admit when and where conflict happens, but also to simply and specifically communicate with each other about conflict—according to the way of Jesus.

After the Teaching: Adequate time is given (with live or recorded music playing) for students to interact with this Prayer Station according to what was just taught. It's always important to walk through the instructions thoroughly, helping the students see the symbolism and the prayer focus that tie into the teaching.

This Prayer Station encourages students to be honest about areas of conflict in relationships—and to humbly and immediately communicate with those they're in conflict with.

Activity/Response: As students approach the Prayer Station, instructions (see sign text on accompanying CD) are given to students to read, as well as the corresponding Scripture passage. More than one student can participate at this station at a time.

Students are invited to write down specific attitudes of theirs that lead to conflicts in their relationships and then to nail these pieces of paper to the cross—symbolically giving the ugliness to Jesus to redeem. They're then encouraged to approach within 48 hours the people with whom they're in conflict—simply and humbly communicating to mend the relationship.

Supplies:
- Table and tablecloth or tapestries
- Instructional signs on 8.5 x 11 paper
- 2 or 3 candles
- 8 to 10 packs of sticky notes (as needed)

- 4 to 8 pens
- Two 2 x 4 boards and nails to create a cross
- Paint (to decorate the cross simply, if desired)
- Long, thick nails—hammered so the sharp end is pointing upward

Setting Up the Station: Place a tablecloth on the table—and put the instructional signs and Scripture passage in multiple places where they can be easily read. Make the cross central on the table. Place sticky notes and pens all around the cross so that multiple people can visit the station simultaneously.

Signs/Directions: On accompanying CD

Relationships: Cutting Out the Bad

Scripture: Matthew 5:29-30

Themes: Conflict in Relationships, Honesty, Forgiveness, Humility, Repentance, Purity, Lust

How to Use This Prayer Station: It directly ties into Jesus' Sermon on the Mount teaching from Matthew 5:29-30 about the importance of dealing with conflict in relationships.

Teaching: Without eliminating wrong attitudes or actions, we cannot change. We become so attached to our habits and routines (which are often destructive to ourselves and others). We often manipulate to get our way and abuse substances or situations that have the potential to be positive and used responsibly. Jesus raises the standard of what the moral laws in Hebrew Scriptures command. He invites us as his followers to be free from our bad habits and routines of easy selfishness and subtle corruption. What's the way out? Admitting our problem and what causes it so we can cut those attitudes or actions out of our daily experiences.

After the Teaching: This Prayer Station encourages students to be honest about areas of conflict in relationships—and to humbly and immediately communicate with those they're in conflict with.

Activity/Response: As students approach the Prayer Station, instructions (see sign text on accompanying CD) are given to students to read, as well as the corresponding Scripture passage. More than one student can participate at this station at a time.

Students are asked to identify what specific attitude or action is bringing harm to themselves or others, then they cut off a piece of yarn—symbolically asking Jesus to cut that attitude or action from their lives. Time can be spent at the station praying afterward, but the focus of this station is to take action, following the teaching of Jesus in removing what's harmful.

Supplies:
- A table and tablecloth or tapestries
- Instructional signs on 8.5 x 11 paper
- 2 or 3 candles
- 4 rolls of yarn

- 4 pairs of scissors
- A basket or vase (for the cut yarn)

Setting Up the Station: Place a tablecloth on the table—and put the instructional signs and Scripture passage in multiple places where they can be easily read. Centrally place the basket or vase for the discarded yarn pieces. Place a roll of yarn beside a set of scissors at four places around the table.

Signs/Directions: On accompanying CD

PART 3

Holiday and Holy Day (and Other) Prayer Experiences from Lilly's Community

The Prayer Experiences in this part can be created on their own for special services or within your regular worship context. That means that the prayer stations in each experience can be used within a worship service with a teaching or sermon, or they can be created where participants come for a special time of prayer and just follow the stations' directions (not as a part of a service with an opening or closing). They also can be created as Prayer Rooms for retreats and special events.

These experiences can be used by all ages and are an amazing opportunity for your church to invite friends and family who don't regularly attend worship services to participate in interactive prayer. They also have time and space to engage God on their own.

Be creative and don't be limited or intimidated by the number of stations in each experience. Feel free to cut and paste and use the ones that fit what your community needs. Also you can choose to do a series for a holiday/holy season and do a couple of stations each week or even recreate a station into a communal response, having the entire congregation or group do the activity/response together.

Art stations (where participants can draw/create their prayers) and rest stations/chill spaces (where participants can stop and be with God along the way) are part of each prayer experience.

The intro stations set up the scene/theme for the event or gathering and introduce the participants to what they're about to do and what they can expect.

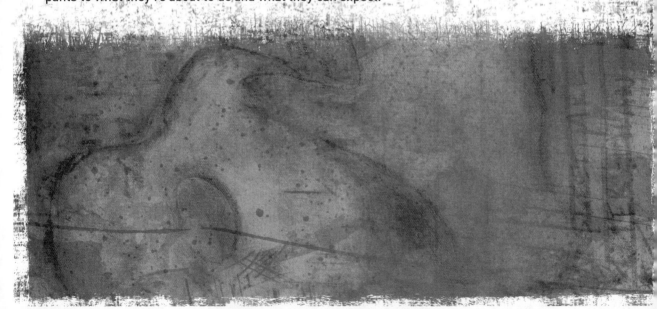

Advent

What Is Advent?

The season of Advent is the four weeks prior to Christmas. According to the church year/calendar, the season of Advent begins the New Year and begins the story of Jesus' life all over again.

The liturgical colors for Advent are purple and dark or royal blue. Purple reminds us of royalty and that this season used to be focused on repentance in addition to the joy of Christ's birth. Many churches now use royal blue to distinguish the season of Advent from the season of Lent, which also uses purple. Colors remind us of the story and help us remember it. The purple of Advent foretells the suffering of Good Friday.

The Advent wreath is a traditional symbol of the season in many denominations/churches. The lighting of an Advent wreath each week during December is part of these worship services. The Advent wreath consists of a circle of evergreen boughs (representing eternal life) and four candles to be lit one at a time (adding a candle each week as the weeks go on). On Christmas a white center candle is added as the Christ candle to signify Jesus' birth. There are various meanings for the candles. I grew up with candles that meant prophet, Bethlehem, shepherd, and angel—but there is also hope, peace, joy, and love. Some church traditions use three purple candles and one pink (signifying joy on week 3).

Rather than having just one person or one family light the candle or candles each week, we wanted everyone to participate in the process, so we created an oversized Advent wreath so everyone could light their own candles as they entered the worship space. One year we used a couple of low tables from the children's ministry area, covered the tables with tablecloths, and created the wreath out of an evergreen garland, placing four large pillar candles around the edges. In the center we placed several glass trays covered in sand and filled them with enough votive candles so everyone had one to light.

We altered the latter another year using a six-foot-wide round table and the same garland idea but with tea lights in glass holders in the center—and thus our candles (our "lights") became the Christ candle. We had the weekly Advent candles lit as people came in, and then we lit our candles after taking Communion.

That year we covered the center of the table with a purple satin cloth to bring in the Advent color. The lighting of our individual candles symbolized several things, depending upon the theme of the day: Willingness to wait on Jesus, willingness to participate in Advent, willingness to give ourselves as gifts to God.

One year we went way outside the box and created the Advent wreath with a kiddie pool! We placed it in the center of the worship space and filled it with water. As people entered the worship space, they lit a floating candle as a symbol of their participation in Advent. This gave us the light of the world and the living water symbols all at the same time! If you haven't participated in the Advent season or followed the church-year calendar, why not give it a try this year?

Prayer Experience
WAITING

(Advent)

Themes: Christmas, Birth of Jesus, Advent, God's timing, Waiting on God, Time, Zechariah and Elizabeth, Mary, Anna and Simeon

Setting Up the Experience: The stations within this experience have a beginning, but they don't necessarily have an exact order for placement in a worship space/room.

We set them up originally around our worship space, but we also included the hallway and entrance area outside our chapel for additional space for stations. We used these stations as the main focus of our worship time, beginning together in a group with an opening prayer and song, and then the sermon was the stations.

The theme of the night was introduced and the prayer/worship time was explained before everyone was invited to participate. We projected slides of nativity paintings (everything from little kid drawings to paintings by the masters) running on a screen during our prayer/worship time for folks to pray with as an additional station.

While these stations don't have an exact order, make sure they're easy to follow, and the traffic flow is good so folks don't get confused or frustrated. We've also used this experience as a special event for an entire week. We set it up on Sunday, and each evening it was open to the public from 7 p.m. to 9 p.m. So there was a definite beginning station and an ending point for folks.

Supplies for General Space: Clocks of various kinds, candles, canvas tarps or other table cloths for table coverings for each station, fabrics to add to decoration of stations in Advent colors: purple, royal blue, gold, etc., Christmas trees, Christmas trees with lights, Christmas mini-lights/tube lights for illuminating the experience (white), candleholders, greenery, manger, wooden stable, manger/nativity scene, art supplies, Chill Space supplies (large pillows, cushions, comfy chairs), instrumental music for backdrop (*Dancing at the Gate* by Dana Cunningham, *Christmas Eve* by David Lanz, *Stars in the Morning East* by Jeff Johnson and Brain Dunning), pizza boxes, Crock-Pot, collection of timers, candles to take home (enough for each participant), pens, small sheets of paper or sticky notes, small candles that individuals can light for the Advent wreath.

Prayer Station 0: Introduction to Advent

Scripture: Psalm 27:14; 40:1-3; (see also Psalm 37:34; 33:20); Micah 5:1-2; Isaiah 9:1-3; 6-7; 11:1-5; Jeremiah 23:5; Luke 2:8-15

Note: Don't feel as though you have to print out all these passages. Less is more. Use the ones you want to focus on, and you can use the other "waiting" Scripture passages later in the Prayer Experience.

Purpose: This station introduces the theme of the worship experience and introduces the concept of Advent.

Activity/Response: Reading and preparation for worship and prayer

Supplies:
- Candles and/or other lighting
- Christmas greenery
- Advent wreath (optional)
- Nativity scene (without Baby Jesus because we are waiting for him) or just the stable (optional)
- Signs and Scripture

Setting Up the Station: This station sets the mood for the Prayer Experience and can contain elements found throughout the other Prayer Stations, such as the stable or an Advent wreath. Cover the table and add lighting as desired; make sure the signs are displayed so they're easily read. Better to keep it simple than to have too many things on this table/space.

Signs/Directions: On accompanying CD

Prayer Station 1: We Don't Like Waiting!

Scripture: Psalm 130; Lamentations 3:25-27

Purpose: To help participants consider how they view waiting and begin to realize that there is a lot of waiting in the Bible.

Activity/Response: Participants will set a timer for three minutes and see if they can wait that long. They will consider what waiting means to them.

Supplies:
- Several timers (egg timers, digital-cooking timers, etc.), with at least a couple that actually can be set and used
- Table and covering
- Lighting
- Signs and Scripture
- Greenery as desired

Setting Up the Station: This station can be set up along with the transitional station prayer signs. Just make sure the signs that tell participants to start the timer are near the timers. Cover the table or base with a table covering. Place signs so they're easily read and followed. Arrange the collection of timers so they're easy to use. Place lighting at the back of the station so it doesn't get in the way of the timers.

Signs/Directions: On accompanying CD

Prayer Station 2: Waiting in the Christmas Story

Scripture: Luke 1:5-25 (Zechariah and Elizabeth); Luke 1:57-80 (Zechariah); Luke 1:26-38 (Mary); Matthew 1:18-25 (Mary and Joseph); Luke 1:39-56 (Mary and Elizabeth)

Purpose: To consider the people who waited in the story of Jesus' birth

Activity/Response: Participants will read the Scripture passages and consider the ways that various people in the Bible waited, specifically those in the Christmas story.

Supplies:
- Printed signs and Scripture (several copies of the Scripture passages could be available)
- Chairs
- Lighting
- Greenery and decoration as space allows and as desired

Setting Up the Station: The signs for this station could be hung on a wall, and you could place two or three chairs facing the signs; the signs could also be taped to the backs of chairs or a pew (to be read as you walk down a row or walk down a hallway), depending on your worship space. This is a station focused on reading Scripture, so a comfortable chair or two will benefit those who'd rather sit than stand to read. Make sure the Scripture is in a large enough font and that there's enough light so the passages are easily read.

Signs/Directions: On accompanying CD

Prayer Station 3: The Survey Says

Scripture: Psalm 27:14; 37:34; 40:1-3

Purpose: Participants will consider various things they wait for and how they view (and how God views) waiting.

Activity/Response: Participants will fill out a survey that will help them consider how they wait. (Note: The survey can also be used as an opening activity before engaging in the worship stations.)

Supplies:
- Surveys, enough copies for the number of participants
- Pens/pencils
- Table and covering
- Lighting as needed
- Chairs
- Clipboards (optional)

Setting Up the Station: This station requires space for writing. You could have several clipboards with the surveys and pens attached. A six-foot table could be used so participants have the space to work. Signs can be hung on the wall above the table or placed on frames along the back or center of the table. You can also run a strand of lights along the back of the table along with greenery if desired. The simplified version is to just place a stack of the surveys and pens/pencils on the table and have participants fill them out elsewhere in the worship space, but the disadvantage to this is that they might not take the time to fill them out.

Signs/Directions: On accompanying CD

Prayer Station 4: How Do You Perceive Time?

Scripture: Ecclesiastes 3:11; Galatians 6:9; Psalm 90:4

Purpose: Participants will consider whose time they're living on and who's running their time. This station will encourage them to live on God's time.

Activity/Response: Participants will consider different kinds of clocks and whose time they're living on. They will be encouraged to use the clocks in their lives to help them focus on living on God's time.

Supplies:
- Collection of various types of clocks, alarm clocks, wall clocks, travel clocks, and watches (a clock with different time zones is really a great addition)
- Signs and Scripture
- Table and covering
- Lighting as needed
- Greenery as desired

Setting Up the Station: Cover the table. Set up a collection of clocks and watches on the table. Use boxes or small bins of various heights and cover them with a cloth, then place clocks on them to give visual variety to the station. Weave white Christmas lights around the clocks to light the station. Hang or place signs so they're easily read.

Signs/Directions: On accompanying CD

Prayer Station 5: Instant Everything—Pizza-Delivery Christianity?

Scripture: Ecclesiastes 3:1-8

Purpose: Participants will consider whether they view God and their spiritual lives as "instant" or "long-cooking." Do they expect God to answer in 30 minutes or less? Or do they know that God's time is God's alone?

Activity/Response: Participants will add to a list their own excuses for not waiting; you can use a spiral notebook for each participant to write in.

Supplies:
- Pizza box or two
- Slow cooker or two
- Pad of paper or photocopied papers run off with "List of Excuses" at the top
- Pen/pencil
- Signs
- Table and covering
- Lighting as needed

Setting Up the Station:
Cover the table with a cloth or tarp. Arrange the station so the pizza boxes and slow cookers are the focus. You can even put the slow cookers on top of the pizza boxes. Arrange or hang the signs so they're easily read. Have the spiral notebook on the table with a pen/pencil so that participants can add their excuses to the list. (You may want to have some excuses already written in the notebook so folks feel welcome to add to it.)

Signs/Directions: On accompanying CD

Prayer Station 6: Taking the Time to Create

Scripture: Exodus 31:1-4; Colossians 3:23

Purpose: Because we're so busy, we often opt out of the process of life. This station gives participants the time and space to create a prayer and to actually participate in the process of creation.

Activity/Response: Participants will create a work of art to hang on a prayer tree.

Supplies:
- Christmas tree (real or artificial) with white Christmas lights
- Hooks
- Mug-sized gift boxes
- Art supplies: scissors, glue, glue sticks, yarn, ribbon, construction paper, markers, etc.
- Squares and circles of tagboard or posterboard with holes punched in the top
- Signs
- Bin/trash can
- Table and covering
- Lighting as needed

Setting Up the Station: This is a station to set up in a corner of the worship area so participants have the space and freedom to be creative. Set up a Christmas tree decorated with white lights. The size of the tree is determined by the size of your group. Set up a table with various art supplies and creative elements. Have a large enough table for folks to actually have room to work. Use your imagination as to what supplies you want to have on the table. Create some examples and hang them on the tree before the worship begins so folks get the idea. Have signs hung or placed so they're easily read. Have someone check on the space throughout the worship time so the table doesn't get junky. Have a container for trash. Light the space as needed in keeping with the theme of the worship space. (Note: This is still worship, so it shouldn't be seen as a place to talk or socialize; this station shouldn't be too far from the rest of the stations but not in the center, so the tree doesn't block everything.)

Signs/Directions: On accompanying CD

Prayer Station 7: Preparing the Way

Scripture: Isaiah 40:2-4; 57:14-15; Mark 1:1-3; Matthew 3:1-3

Purpose: This station gives participants an opportunity to confess and consider the junk in their lives that blocks them from being ready for King Jesus.

Activity/Response: Participants will play in the sand, hold rocks, take rocks out of the sand and out of the bin, and pray about what things block them and clog up their paths to God.

Supplies:
- Dishpan, tub, or small storage bin (two or three bins if you have a large group)
- Sand
- Rocks, small stones
- Signs and Scripture
- Table and covering
- Lighting as needed

Setting Up the Station: Cover the table/base with a tarp or cloth. Fill the dishpan/tub with sand about half to three-quarters full. Place several stones of various sizes in the bin. If you have a larger group participating, you can use more than one bin—just duplicate. Place signs so they're easy to read and make sense to the participants. If you use more than one bin, provide enough space between them so participants have a little privacy and elbow room. If you have two bins of sand, you may want to duplicate the signs, too. Light the station as desired. You can even place a candle in a glass holder in the bin if you have the room, or arrange a length of white Christmas lights behind or around the bins of sand.

Signs/Directions: On accompanying CD

Prayer Station 8: Who Are You Waiting For?

Scripture: Matthew 7:6-8; Luke 11:9-11

Purpose: This station allows each person to engage with God and the Christmas season.

Activity/Response: Participants will put their names on pieces of paper or sticky notes and place them in a manger or a manger scene/stable as they tell Jesus what they need during Christmas.

Supplies:
- Large wooden manger or a stable from a nativity scene (no human figures)
- Small squares of paper (gold/yellow) or sticky notes in different colors
- Basket for paper and pens
- Straw for manger
- Pens
- Signs and Scripture
- Table and covering
- Lighting as needed

Setting Up the Station: If you have a large wooden manger, organize the station around it with a small table set up with the pens and paper on it. If you use a stable from a nativity scene, place this on a table covered with a cloth and have the paper and pens nearby. Hang or place the signs so they're easily read and followed. Light the station as needed.

Signs/Directions: On accompanying CD

Prayer Station 9: Willing to Wait on Emmanuel

Scripture: John 1:14

Purpose: At this station, participants create a visual symbol of their willingness to wait during the season of Advent/Christmas and be part of what God is doing.

Activity/Response: Participants will light candles and add them to the center of the Advent wreath, and they will take home a candle to remind them that God is with them during the Advent/Christmas season.

Supplies:
- Four large candleholders for Advent candles
- Circle of greenery
- Trays or some kind of base to place individual candles on (we used glass trays covered in sand with tea lights or votive candles)
- Candles to give away to participants (any type of candle is fine, depending upon what you can get donated or acquire inexpensively)
- Basket for candles as needed
- Table with covering; a round table works best
- Lighters for candles
- Signs and Scripture

Setting Up the Station: Cover a round table with a cloth. Create a large Advent wreath with a space in the middle big enough for the number of candles for your group; if your group is too large for this, you'll need to have someone blow out some candles as participants move through the stations so they'll all have candles to light. Candles should be placed on an appropriate base so table or tablecloth isn't damaged by wax. Place two to four lighters around the wreath. Place candles to take home in a basket near the wreath and the directional sign. If needed, place the candles to take home on another small table near the Advent wreath.

Signs/Directions: On accompanying CD

Prayer Station 10: Missing the Gift

Scripture: John 13:34; Matthew 28:19-20; John 3:16

Purpose: This station gives participants the opportunity to pray for others.

Activity/Response: Participants will write down the names of friends and family members who need to know the love of God this season—those who are waiting to know Jesus. They'll put these names on gift tags and hang the tags on a Christmas tree illuminated with only white lights. (Option: You can use gift tags—the sticker type—and have participants place them on a large gift box or bag.)

Supplies:
- Gift tags; you can create your own or purchase the types of tags with a fold and a string for hanging. You can also purchase boxed Christmas cards at the dollar store and punch a hole in the corners so they can be hung on the tree.
- Christmas tree decorated with only white lights
- Hooks, if needed
- Pens
- Basket for tags
- Optional: Large gift bag stuffed so it stands open or a wrapped gift box and sticker-type gift tags instead of hanging ones
- Table and covering
- Lighting as desired
- Signs and Scripture

Setting Up the Station:
Choice 1: Set up a Christmas tree covered with white lights. Set up a table with a basket filled with gift tags and pens and ribbons/string to hang them with or Christmas tree hooks for hanging the tags or Christmas cards. Provide enough room on the table for writing on tags/cards.
Choice 2: Cover a table with a tablecloth and cover the top of the table with a piece of wrapping paper or brown butcher paper. Place on the table a large gift bag or gift box wrapped in plain paper. Have a basket filled with sticker tags on the table and space on the table to write. Provide pens for filling out tags. (Note: In both cases hang signs on the wall behind the table. Illuminate the table with small white lights.)

Signs/Directions: On accompanying CD

Prayer Station 11: Types of Waiting

Scripture: Luke 2:21-35; 36-40

Purpose: Participants will get to know the stories of two people who waited on God's timing—Anna and Simeon. They'll also look closely at how they themselves wait and at two types of waiting—active and still.

Activity/Response: Participants will read the stories of Simeon and Anna and consider what it means to wait on God's timing. They will get a Tootsie Pop to take home or eat as a part of the station.

Supplies:
- Tootsie Pops, enough for all participants
- Basket to hold candy
- Scripture passages on Anna and Simeon, printed in large font
- Signs
- Table and covering as needed
- Lighting as needed
- Chairs or cushions for seating

Setting Up the Station: This is a reading station, so there can be chairs used as a part of the setup and a small table on which to place the candy. The signs can be hung on the wall with the chairs facing in. Make sure there's enough lighting for reading. This station also can be on a pew or a row of chairs—or you could use large floor pillows/cushions for sitting, rather than chairs.

Signs/Directions: On accompanying CD

Prayer Station 12: Chill Space

Scripture: Psalm 46:10

Purpose: This station provides participants a place to stop and rest and actually take the time to wait on God.

Activity/Response: Participants will sit in a quiet, comfortable place and have time to be with God and the option to rest, reflect, pray, and journal.

Supplies:
- Large pillows, cushions, beanbag chairs, etc.
- Comfy floor covering
- Spiral notebooks, journals, pens, pencils, or just paper and pens
- Bibles
- Desk lamps and small lamps for soft lighting
- Signs

Setting Up the Station:
Create a space that's restful and comfortable. Fill the space with large floor pillows, beanbag chairs, pillows, comfortable floor coverings, etc. There could also be "real" comfortable chairs as you have space. The idea is to create a restful oasis where participants can spend time in prayer and journaling. Set up some soft lighting such as small bedside-type lamps or desk lamps focused away from the space. Have a small table with Bibles, journals, and paper and pens available, and place the signs where they can be easily read.

Signs/Directions: On accompanying CD

Prayer Experience
FOLLOWING THE STAR

(Advent, Christmas, or Epiphany) *Epiphany commences on January 6 and celebrates the manifestation of God in human form—specifically the Maji's visit to the infant Jesus.

Themes: Advent, Christmas, Epiphany, drawing closer to God, following Jesus, being a light to the world, praying for our world and ourselves

General Supplies: Collection of stars, star ornaments, light-up stars, nativity scenes, magi, ladder, gold glitter, treasure chest, vessels that could hold frankincense and myrrh, sticky-note stars, sheets of stars, candles, one set of scented candles or mild incense, craft foam stars, map of the world, collection of flashlights and batteries, various types of salt, votive candles for individuals to light, large platters as bases for votive candles, table coverings, tarps, velvet/satin cloths, rope lighting, white Christmas lights, candles for lighting

Prayer Station 0: Getting Ready for the Journey

Scripture: Matthew 2:1-12

Purpose: Introduces participants to the theme of the worship time and is designed to help participants prepare for the prayer journey they're about to begin.

Note: The text connected to this station could be read aloud to the entire group, or it could be handed out to each person rather than set up as a station.

Activity/Response: The focus is on reading. Participants are invited to take off their shoes and read Matthew 2:1-12.

Supplies:
- Table and covering
- 2 easels or picture frames
- Velvet or satin cloth that adds to "wise men/magi" flavor of setting
- Candles for decoration in glass holders
- Copies or one enlarged copy of Matthew 2:1-12 and the opening sign

Setting Up the Station: Provide a place for participants to remove their shoes. Have several copies of Matthew 2:1-12 or one enlarged copy of text. The text and the sign could both be enlarged and set up on an easel or in frames on a table with candles beside them, saving props for the next station. If a table is used, cover it with a cloth and perhaps a rich fabric such as velvet or satin to set the tone of the journey of the wise men/magi. This fabric can be the tablecloth or it could be draped around the signs or candles. Make sure the candles are in glass containers.

Signs/Directions: On accompanying CD

Prayer Station 1: The Quest of the Magi

Scripture: Matthew 2

Purpose: Participants will consider being current-day magi.

Activity/Response: Participants will read "The Quest of the Magi" meditation and then stamp their hands with a star stamp. Note: This meditation could be printed on a sign at a station so it can be considered individually, or it could be handed out to each person as they arrive. Or "The Quest of the Magi" could be read aloud to the entire group before the prayer experience begins, before folks go pray at the stations.

Supplies:
- Star rubber stamp and a stamp pad (gold, red, some color that will show up on skin); you might need more than one if you have a large group.
- Treasure box, incense holder, decorative jar that might hold myrrh
- Large star
- Candles for decoration
- Table and table covering
- Other lighting as needed
- Signs

Setting Up the Station: Decorate a table with a covering and elements of the journey, which could be a treasure box, incense, a jar for myrrh, candles, a large gold star, etc. Have a stack of "The Quest of the Magi" meditations run off or have an enlarged version so it's easy to read by more than one person. Place the star stamp and stamp pad to the side of the "Quest" stack. Place the signs so they're easy to read and follow. Put a piece of paper or an old piece of cloth under the stamp pads to save the tablecloth from ink.

Signs/Directions: On accompanying CD

Prayer Station 2: Stuck in the Palace

Scripture: Matthew 2:1-12, 1 John 1:8-10

Purpose: This station gives participants an opportunity to confess the junk that keeps them "stuck in the palace"—the things that block them from Jesus.

Activity/Response: On pieces of duct tape participants will write down the fears, blocks, sins, etc., that keep them from going to worship, the things that keep them "stuck," the things that keep them from following the star.

Supplies:
- Duct tape (silver), two rolls
- Old chair that can have duct tape placed on it (or old sheet). See set-up.
- Black Sharpie markers
- Straw/Hay
- Figure of Jesus in the manger
- Tray or basket to hold straw
- Signs and Scripture

Setting Up the Station: Cover an old chair in duct tape so the tape is actually sticky to sit on. If you don't have a chair that can be directly taped onto, then cover a chair with a sheet and make enough loops of duct tape to stick all over the chair.

Cover a tray or fill a shallow bin with straw. (We've used a cookie sheet and covered it with straw and placed our duct tape in the straw; another time we used a kid's easel with extensions to hang the tape.) Place a "Jesus in the manger" figure on the straw. Another option is to cover a small tabletop with the straw and place the "Jesus in the manger" figure in the middle. The participants will put their tape pieces around the figure. Provide a few cut or torn strips of duct tape ready to go. Provide small scissors for cutting of tape. Place a basket with scissors, tape, and Sharpie markers on the table or near the straw. Place the signs where they're easily read and followed. You can hang the signs on the wall and face the chair toward them. Make sure the signs are placed in a way that makes sense for them to be followed.

Signs/Directions: On accompanying CD

Prayer Station 3: Light of the World

Scripture: John 8:12; Matthew 4:16; Isaiah 9:2; Matthew 5:43-45

Purpose: Gives participants an opportunity to pray for our world, specific countries, missionaries, as well as our enemies.

Activity/Response: Participants will place sticky stars on a map of the world and pray for specific countries and people.

Supplies:
- Large map of the world
- Sticky-note stars (a pad of sticky notes shaped as a star), or cut out stars from yellow paper and use tape.
- Black Sharpie markers
- Basket to hold stars and markers
- Signs and Scripture
- Lighting as desired

Setting Up the Station: The map of the world can be hung on a wall or spread on a table. Have a small table covered with a cloth, or cover a stool with a cloth, and have a basket filled with the star pads (stars and tape) and markers. Create some example stars and place them on the map. Hang signs or place signs around the map so they're easy to read and follow. Use lighting as desired. If the map is on a table, candles or rope lighting could be set up around the map.

Signs/Directions: On accompanying CD

Prayer Station 4: Following the Star (part 1)

Scripture: Hebrews 12:1-2: Psalm 32:8

Purpose: Participants will consider what they need to do more of (or less of) in order to follow the star of Jesus in the new year.

Activity/Response: Participants will write down on sheets of stars the things they need to do less of and the things they need to do more of in the coming year in order to follow the star and live for Jesus. They'll place their stars in the manger and take home a copy of these stars to remind them of what they did and how they can follow Jesus' star in the new year.

Optional: Take home a craft foam star as a reminder.

Supplies:
- Manger filled with straw or a manger/nativity scene
- Photocopied sheets of stars (two sheets of stars for each participant...four large stars on each sheet)
- Scissors, four pair
- Sharpie markers
- Optional: Craft foam stars to take home (enough for the entire group)
- Basket for foam stars
- Basket for markers and scissors
- Lighting as desired (rope lighting for a large manger; or small white Christmas lights around a manger scene highlighting the station)
- Table covering as needed

Signs/Directions: On accompanying CD

Prayer Station 5: Following the Star (part 2)

Scripture: James 4:7-8; Jeremiah 29:13-14; Deuteronomy 31:6; Matthew 28:20

Purpose: Participants will use the ladder as their gauge for where they are with Jesus. They will pray about their closeness to Jesus.

Activity/Response: They will place sticky stars on the ladder to show how close or far away from Jesus they feel.

Supplies:
- Ladder (6 ft. to 8 ft.)
- Sticky-note stars or sticker stars; or create your own with paper and tape
- Sharpie markers
- Lighting
- Signs
- Basket for stars and markers

Signs/Directions: On accompanying CD

Prayer Station 6: Salt and Light

Scripture: Matthew 5:13-15 (TNIV and *The Message*); John 12:44-46; John 1:1-12; 8:12

Purpose: This station gives participants a chance to consider being a light to others and receiving God's light personally. It also gives them an opportunity to pray for friends who need God's love and light.

Activity/Response: Participants will look at various flashlights while also considering how they themselves shine their own lights for Jesus in their worlds. They will pray for friends who need the light of Jesus by writing down their names on a picture of a flashlight they'll take home with them as a prayer reminder. Finally they'll taste salt as a reminder that Jesus calls us to be salt of the earth, as well as light.

Supplies:
- Collection of flashlights—a few with bright lights and a few with weak batteries
- Collection of various sizes and types of batteries
- Small basket a flashlight would fit under
- Trays of small candles
- Lighters
- Salt packets like you'd find at a fast-food chain, salt boxes, etc., and salt in a container to taste
- Photos or drawings of a flashlight (enough for more than the number of participants)
- Basket to hold printed copies of flashlights
- Pens
- Table and covering
- Lighting
- Signs and Scripture

Setting Up the Station: This station has multiple parts. You'll need a long table or two or three smaller tables set up together. You can also use a pew base for this station with the back of the pew for hanging the signs. Arrange the collection of flashlights and the basket along with the signs that talk about what kind of light you have.

The second piece of the station is the salt tasting. Place various types of salt packages around a dish of salt to taste. Then place trays of candles and a couple of lighters next to it. Finally provide room for pens and the stack or basket of photos or drawings of flashlights, along with the signs about whom the participants will pray for. Make sure there's space for writing.

Signs/Directions: On accompanying CD

Prayer Station 7: The Oasis

Scripture: Psalm 46:10; Matthew 11:28

Purpose: This station provides a mini-Sabbath—an opportunity to rest along the journey.

Activity/Response: Participants can sit and pray, read the Bible, journal their prayers, or just rest and BE with God.

Supplies:
- Large floor cushions/pillows
- Spiral notebooks, composition books, journals
- Pens/pencils
- Comfortable floor covering
- Optional: Tent set up with large floor pillows, cushions
- Plants

Setting Up the Station: Create a restful place where participants can sit and pray and be with Jesus. If your worship space is large enough, you might want to set up a tent as your oasis/chill space. The cushions and floor coverings would be set up inside the tent. Just make sure you monitor for "purpling" (i.e., let everyone know ahead of time that this is a worship space, not a dating space).

Signs/Directions: On accompanying CD

Prayer Station 8: Art

Scripture: James 1:16-18; Exodus 31:1-5

Purpose: This station provides a place where participants can create tactile prayers; this is an opportunity to pray with art and writing.

Activity/Response: Participants will create their prayers for Jesus through art and writing.

Supplies:
- Art supplies such as colored pencils, crayons, oil pastels, charcoal/drawing pencils, markers of various colors and sizes
- Various kinds of paper (e.g., construction paper, drawing paper, sketch pads, white paper)
- Journals or spiral notebooks
- Blue painter's tape to hang up creations
- Tape, glue sticks, scissors

Setting Up the Station: Provide a table set up for art and writing. Have art supplies and paper available with space to create. Chairs will be needed at this station. Create some examples and use blue painter's tape to hang them so others can follow. Hang the sign so it's easily read.

Signs/Directions: On accompanying CD

Prayer Station 9: Breathing Grace

Scripture: Genesis 2:4-7; John 20:21-22; Ephesians 2:8-9; 5:1-2

Purpose: Participants will consider breathing in the fragrance of God.

Action/Response: Participants will read the "Sense of Breathing" meditation (available on CD) and breathe in the fragrance of the candles/incense.

Supplies:
- Gold glitter
- Candles with a rich scent (or a mild incense)
- Three wise men/magi figures
- Copy of the "Sense of Breathing" meditation (enlarged if desired)
- Table and covering
- Other lighting as needed

Setting Up the Station: Cover the table with a cloth and place the "Sense of Breathing" meditation on it with the candles/incense close by. Surround the reading with gold glitter.

Signs/Directions: On accompanying CD

Prayer Experience
JOURNEY TO THE CROSS

(Holy Week)

Journey to the Cross was envisioned as a stand-alone Prayer Experience, to which we invited our entire congregation (and their friends) as participants. Several churches have used Journey to the Cross as part of their Holy Week worship. We set up this worship experience so that people came each evening during the week from 7 p.m. to 9 p.m., and they began with Station 0 and continued to the closing Station 12. The stations are in order, telling the story of the last week of Jesus' life, leading finally to the cross. This experience can be used by all ages and is a great opportunity for your church to invite friends and family who might not regularly attend worship services.

Themes: Easter, Holy Week, Crucifixion, Last Week of Christ's Life, Forgiveness

Purpose: This station takes participants on a journey from Jesus' triumphal entry into Jerusalem on Palm Sunday through the events of the last week of Jesus' life, ending with the Crucifixion and the hope of the new life that is to come on Easter Sunday. The Journey to the Cross consists of 12 Prayer Stations (plus the intro, Station 0) that will provide participants with an interactive, multisensory opportunity to reflect on the last week in the life of Jesus and a time of quiet in the midst of their busy lives.

General Supplies: Rope lighting and small white Christmas lights, candles in glass containers (preferably white and unscented, except for the Gethsemane station), table coverings (e.g., canvas tarps, muslin, etc.), Sharpie markers (black and multiple colors), pens and watercolor markers, large wooden cross

Prayer Station 0: Introduction

Purpose: The focus of this station is to introduce participants to the themes of Journey to the Cross and help them prepare for it.

Activity/Response: Participants will read signs before heading to Station 1.

Supplies:

- Signs
- Ziplock baggies to store "take-aways" from each of the stations

Setting Up the Station: Create enough space for multiple participants to read the signs and directions and explanations at once. Simplicity and plenty of room are the keys.

Signs/Directions: On accompanying CD

Prayer Station 1: Last Week on Earth

Scripture: Proverbs 3:5-6; Jeremiah 29:11-13

Purpose: The focus of this station is to meditate on the last week in the life of Jesus and then reflect on one's own life. What would participants do if they only had a week to live?

Activity/Response: Participants will write a postcard describing what they'd do and where they'd be if they only had one week to live.

Supplies:
- Photocopied or printed postcards on 8.5 x 11 paper in bright colors; one side looks like a postcard with a stamp in the corner; the other side has a photo. You can use photos from old calendars, travel pictures, etc., to create the photo side.
- Pens
- Table with tablecloth
- Signs/Instructions
- Lighting as desired

Setting Up the Station: Cover the table with a tablecloth or other covering. Create a space with enough room to write. Provide a stack of postcards (see the supply list for instructions on making these), pens, and signs. Highlight the station with lighting as desired.

Signs/Directions: On accompanying CD

Prayer Station 2: Triumphal Entry (Palm Sunday Reflection)

Scripture: Mark 11:1-19; Luke 19:28-40; John 12:12-19; Matthew 21:1-11; Zechariah 9:9; Psalm 118:25-26; Zephaniah 3:15

Purpose: This station allows participants to consider the triumphal entry of Jesus into Jerusalem and provides an opportunity for them to express praise and thanksgiving to Jesus.

Activity/Response: Participants will walk down a path set up to remind them of the triumphal entry/Palm Sunday, and they will write their prayers and praises on palm branches run off on green paper.

Supplies:
- Brown butcher paper or a roll of brown packing paper
- Artificial or "live" palm branches
- Small stones or rocks can be purchased at a dollar store or craft store
- Run off palm branches on green paper on which participants can write
- Pens or markers
- Sign sets 1 and 2 (there are two sets of signs for this station; you may choose to use one or both)
- Frames for signs so they can be placed along the path, or the signs can be laid along the path on the floor—but in this case they should be laminated.

Setting Up the Station: Create a path using brown butcher paper. Cover the path with palm branches and coats (you can use garments that look like they're from Jesus' time, as well as contemporary coats and jackets) and stones and rocks of different sizes. Place signs along the path so they're easily read and followed. Highlight the path with rope lighting or other lighting as needed.

Signs/Directions: On accompanying CD

Prayer Station 3: Clearing the Temple

Scripture: Luke 19:45-48; Matthew 21:12-17; Romans 8:35-39

Purpose: The focus of this station is to have participants consider the scene of Jesus kicking the moneychangers out of the temple. It will allow the participants to consider and pray about the things that clutter their own hearts and prevent them from worshiping Jesus. Also, participants will consider the folks we keep out of our worship due to prejudice, fear, etc.

Activity/Response: Participants will pray about what things clutter the temples of their hearts and who they keep out of church. They'll hold a coin and consider the clutter in their lives, and they will take home a coin to remind them to pray for the people they've left out and to remind them to make room for Jesus in their hearts.

Supplies:
- Plastic coins or pennies and other change
- Clay pots, baskets
- Small chest with coins, wooden birdcage, etc.
- Signs
- Table and covering and a small table turned over

Setting Up the Station: Create a station that looks like a money changer's table turned over by Jesus. Place clay pots on the floor, money strewn around, etc. Have a basket or chest with plastic coins that participants can take home with them. Hang or place signs so they're easily read and followed. Light the station as needed.

Signs/Directions: On accompanying CD

Prayer Station 4: Jesus Anointed at Bethany

Scripture: John 12:1-11

Purpose: The focus of this station is the extravagant gift of love the woman gave Jesus by anointing him with oil and wiping his feet with her hair. Participants will pray about the things they value the most and about their willingness to give that same kind of extravagant love to Jesus.

Activity/Response: Participants will pour out a sweet-smelling liquid into a bowl and dip a piece of towel into the liquid. They will get to take away the piece of towel as a reminder to express extravagant love for Jesus on a regular basis.

Supplies:
- Ceramic bowl
- Fancy pitcher, vase, vial—something that looks like a perfume bottle
- Soap (lavender liquid hand soap works well)
- White towel
- White terry cloth fabric or a towel cut into small squares (1 x 1- or 1 x 2-inch squares)
- Basket to hold pieces of towel
- Signs
- Table and covering

Setting Up the Station: Cover a table and place the bowl and pitcher on the table. Fill the pitcher ahead of time with some type of good-smelling, thick liquid soap. Ahead of time, cut up a white terry cloth towel into small squares and place these in a basket near the bowl. Before worship begins, pour some of the liquid into the bowl. Place another hand towel by the bowl so participants can wipe their hands if needed.

Signs/Directions: On accompanying CD

Prayer Station 5: The Last Supper…in the Upper Room

Scripture: John 13:1-17; Luke 22:7-30; Exodus 12:17-30; Matthew 26:27-30; Luke 22:14-21

Purpose: This station will help participants engage in the happenings in the upper room on the night of the Last Supper. They'll look at the foot washing and what Passover is, and they'll write about what Jesus' sacrifice means to them.

Activity/Response: (This station has three parts and one optional part.)
In part 1, participants will imagine themselves in the upper room and picture what this would look like and feel like. They'll touch water in a basin/bowl and then wash their hands to remind them of Jesus washing them clean like he washed the disciples' feet. (Optional: You can use a picture or painting of the Last Supper, such as Bohdan Piasecki's, which includes women and children, like a true Passover meal.)

In the second part of the station, they'll read about the Passover and see how it fits together with the Last Supper.

In the final piece of this station (which I create as the main focus of this station), participants will write their prayers and thanksgivings on the table—right on the table cloth. (Note: This tablecloth can be used again for a Communion cloth or altar cloth when you celebrate Communion together.)

For the optional station, participants can take Communion and read about the experience from Scripture.

Supplies:
- Long table set up low to the ground
- Floor pillows or cushions
- Light-colored table cloth or canvas drop cloth that can be written on
- Sharpie pens in various colors
- Chalice/wine glass and a basket with bread
- Signs and Scripture
- Additional table needed for basin and towel portion

- Candles to light the station and additional lighting as needed
- Basin (ceramic bowl) filled with water
- Towels
- Extra water bowls and towels to replace the original water as it gets used and dirty; you can also use paper towels rather than cloth
- Optional: Painting or picture of the Last Supper (preferably not Da Vinci's—Bohdan Piasecki's painting of the Last Supper is a great choice, however).
- Optional: Bread to eat; grape juice to drink

Setting Up the Station: Set up a station that approximates what the upper room, ready for the Last Supper, may have looked like. Use a low table or a table on blocks (plastic storage bins work well as supports under a table, too) so it's no more than two feet off the ground. Cover the table in a cream-colored sheet, tablecloth, or canvas drop cloth that can be written on. Place floor cushions around the table. Spread out Sharpies on the table and write a few sample prayers so others know what to do. Place signs so they're easily read, and place candles on the table. If you have room, on a corner of the table place the wine goblet or chalice, grape juice, and bread to remind people of the Last Supper. These elements could be placed on another table nearby. Create another space nearby with a smaller table for the basin and towels and provide a chair to sit in (and use the optional painting as a focal point). If your denomination/ church will allow it, you can have bread (flat bread, pita bread, etc.) for participants to eat and grape juice to drink as a reminder of Communion and the Last Supper.

Signs/Directions: On accompanying CD

Prayer Station 6: The Garden of Gethsemane

(Adapted from page 97 of Jonny Baker and Doug Gay's book, *Alternative Worship*; used with permission.)

Scripture: Luke 22:39-46; Mark 14:32-42; Matthew 25:34-40

Purpose: This station invites participants to pray for those suffering around the world as they consider the suffering of Jesus.

Activity/Response: Participants will look at photos of global poverty and suffering and pray for both local and global sufferers; they'll also taste the cup of suffering by drinking a sip of red-wine vinegar.

Supplies:
- Pictures of suffering around the globe, cut out from magazines/newspapers or downloaded from the Internet
- Plants, artificial or real
- 2 coffee mugs or cups that can be written on
- Ceramic pen/marker
- Red-wine vinegar
- Signs and Scripture
- Small white Christmas lights and candles as desired
- Table and covering

Setting Up the Station: Set up the station with a covered table. Arrange a couple of plants or an ivy-like artificial garland around the back of the station to capture the garden feeling. Arrange a collage of photos of suffering around the world. Place two mugs or cups on the table. Write on these ahead of time with a ceramic marker: Cup of Suffering. Pour in red-wine vinegar, about half full. Highlight the photos with white Christmas lights or candles. Make sure signs and Scripture are easily read and followed.

Signs/Directions: On accompanying CD

Prayer Station 7: Betrayal and Denial—Judas and Peter

Scripture: Luke 22:1-6; 47-53; 54-62

Purpose: Participants will consider times they've been betrayed and times they've betrayed others. They'll also pray about how they've personally betrayed Jesus.

Activity/Response: Participants will write their names on a "kiss" and put it on a picture of Jesus or on the word *Jesus*.

Supplies:
- Cut-out lips/kisses or you can use "lip" sticky notes if you can find them; (or you can have someone draw a pair of lips shaped like a kiss, photocopy sheets of these on pink paper, and have someone cut out the individual lips); have enough for at least one per person
- Basket for lip cutouts
- Pens
- Tape, if not using sticky notes
- Picture or poster of Jesus, or you can use a poster with *Jesus* written on it and folks can put their kisses on the name *Jesus*
- Signs and Scripture
- Table and covering as needed
- Lighting as needed

Setting Up the Station: Hang a poster of Jesus on a wall or place it flat on a table. Place a basket of kiss cutouts and tape (or "kiss" sticky notes) and pens near the poster. Hang or place signs around the poster so they're easily read and followed. Light the station as needed depending on how you set up the poster.

Signs/Directions: On accompanying CD

Prayer Station 8: Jesus Before Pilate

Scripture: Matthew 25:39-41; 27:11-26; John 9:4-6; 14:5-7

Purpose: Pilate and the Pharisees failed to recognize Jesus for who he really is—the way, the truth, and the life. They had the Light of the World standing before them. But they were blind to him because of their pride and desire for power. The purpose of this station is to help participants realize that sometimes we, too, miss Jesus and don't recognize him in our own lives and in the lives of others.

Activity/Response: Participants will light candles as they pray about recognizing the Light of the World in their lives and in the lives of others.

Supplies:
- Bowl and towel (representing Pilate washing his hands)
- Sand
- Plates or trays (covered in sand)
- Votive or tea light candles, enough for everyone to light (or blow out some candles after they're used once as folks come through the experience so there will be some free to light for others)
- Lighters
- Signs and Scripture
- Optional: Chair that looks like a throne

Setting Up the Station: Cover a table with tablecloth/canvas; place trays with sand, candles, and lighters on the table. If you have a throne-like chair, place it to the side of the table and place the bowl and towel either on the chair or on the corner of the table to remind participants that Pilate washed his hands of Jesus' death. Hang or place signs so they're easily read and followed.

Signs/Directions: On accompanying CD

Stations 9, 10, and 11 are all focused on Jesus' death on the cross. They should be set up next to each other with a large wooden cross at the center or at least as the focal point for the stations. The seven last words of Jesus should be nailed or tacked to the cross. Highlight the station with rope lights and candles. Provide a space at the foot of the cross for a pile of Popsicle-stick crosses that will be made in Station 9.

Prayer Station 9: Forgiveness

Scripture: 1 John 1:8-9

Purpose: The focus of this station is forgiveness. We are forgiven because of Jesus' death on the cross. This station gives participants a chance to ask Jesus to forgive them, and they're also able to ask Jesus to help them forgive others.

Activity/Response: Participants will read the powerful poem "God on a Stick" by Paul Hobbs (which can be found on the CD) and then make crosses from Popsicle sticks using yarn or duct tape. They'll write on the Popsicle-stick cross the name, or names, of folks they need to forgive, then leave it at the foot of the larger cross, or at the station at the base of a smaller cross. (Optional: Take home a copy of the poem.)

Supplies:
- Enlarged text of poem "God on a Stick"
- Text of the poem "God on a Stick" for participants
- Popsicle/craft sticks
- Duct tape
- Pieces of yarn
- Sharpie pens
- Basket for supplies
- Small scissors for cutting yarn
- Table and covering
- Lighting as needed
- Cross, if your station is not close to the large cross

Setting Up the Station: Make the "God on a Stick" poem available for participants on the table or hanging nearby so it's easy to read; if you're making the poem available for participants, have the text on paper on or near the table. Have enough room on the table so participants can construct crosses and write on them. Cover the art table. Place a basket on the table filled with Popsicle sticks, tape or yarn, markers, and scissors. Make two or three example crosses using the duct tape or yarn to connect the Popsicle sticks to make a cross. The participants will decide whether to use yarn or tape to construct their own crosses. Place an example cross or two at the foot of the large wooden cross or provide an additional cross at this station for this purpose. Light the station as needed.

Signs/Directions: On accompanying CD

Prayer Station 10: The Words from the Cross…

Scripture: Luke 23:34, 43; John 19:26-27, Mark 15:34, John 19:28, 30; Luke 23:46

Purpose: This station looks at the final words of Jesus and allows participants to really consider what Jesus did on the cross.

Activity/Response: Participants will read the words Jesus spoke from the cross and pray about what they need Jesus to say to them today.

Supplies:
- Large wooden cross
- Last words of Jesus nailed or tacked on the cross
- Lighting, such as rope lighting, to highlight the cross
- Signs and Scripture

Setting Up the Station: Set up a large wooden cross, the bigger the better. Print out the verses containing the last words of Jesus and hammer or tack them to the cross. Highlight the cross with lighting and candles and have the signs placed so they're easy to read and follow.

Signs/Directions: On accompanying CD

Prayer Station 11: Tearing the Temple Curtain

Scripture: Mark 15:37-38; Luke 23:44-46; Matthew 27:50-52

Purpose: Jesus' death on the cross opens our relationship with God. We now have direct access to God the Father through God the Son. We no longer need priests or sacrifices because Jesus was the sacrifice. He paid the price we couldn't pay. This station reminds us of this fact.

Activity/Response: Participants will rip a piece of cloth to remind them that because of Jesus' death on the cross they're no longer separated from God.

Supplies:
- Squares of purple cotton fabric, precut at one end, enough for the number of participants
- Basket to hold fabric squares
- Signs and Scripture
- Lighting as needed

Setting Up the Station: Set up a table near the large wooden cross. Place a basket filled with pieces of purple fabric, precut on one end, on the table along with the Scripture and the signs. Light the station as needed.

Signs/Directions: On accompanying CD

Prayer Station 12: Plant a Seed

Scripture: Matthew 20:18-20; John 12:23-25

Purpose: The purpose of this station is to remind participants that Jesus said he would rise again and to provide the hope of the resurrection, that there will be an Easter Sunday after the sadness of Good Friday.

Activity/Response: Participants will plant seeds in a flower pot or window box as reminders that Jesus said he's the resurrection and the life.

Supplies:
- Large flowerpot or window box filled with potting soil
- Garden gloves, trowels, seed packets
- Sunflower seed or other larger seeds easily planted, enough for all participants
- Signs and Scripture
- Living plants or flowers for decoration
- Lighting as desired

Setting Up the Station: Cover a table. Place the flowerpot or window box on the table and the seeds close by so they're easily planted. Use seed packets, gloves, etc., as decorations as desired. Make sure signs are easily read and light the station as desired.

Sign/Directions: On accompanying CD

Prayer Experience
TABLES

Themes: Conversations around the Table, Tables where Jesus Sat, Tables of Healing and Reconciliation, Jesus Challenges Us to Live Out His Kingdom

The initial prayer station for this experience comes from Psalm 23. During a conversation and brainstorming session with Jeannie Oestreicher and Larry Warner for a youth worker Sabbath retreat, we discussed the concept of God preparing a table for us in the presence of our enemies—and what this really might mean. Most of the time I'd thought it meant a lavish table where I sat, and my enemies just had to stand around and watch me enjoy it. Larry brought up the concept of sitting down *across* from our enemies and that God prepares a table of reconciliation.

Once I had the Psalm 23 table designed, this got me thinking about all the tables in the Bible, specifically the tables where Jesus sat. Jesus had many amazing conversations around tables, and he also told stories about other people at tables. In the Jewish culture—and in Eastern culture today—eating together is a sign of friendship and hospitality. Around the table is where life happens and relationships are built.

This worship experience first took place on a Sunday evening with pastors and leaders who'd journeyed together over a three-year period, but it can be easily done with students. The Gospel reading for that night was Luke 14:12-24 and the Prayer Stations were the sermon. I've also used Luke 24:13-33 (the road to Emmaus story) as the primary text.

Note: You can use any of the "table" Scripture passages as your main text/focus and have the other stations support the main one. Or you can use a station a week as a response to a teaching/sermon in a series based on the "Tables where Jesus Sat" or "Conversations around the Table." You can also consider other tables where Jesus sat and create your own stations from these passages…or even check out tables in the Old Testament…or consider a station involving tables where we sit every day, such as the lunch table, office tables/desks, dinner table, table in a food court/restaurant where we need to bring the love of Jesus and reconciliation and healing and loving conversation.

Other Notes: We began our worship with an original prayer prayed in unison. We used "Benediction," a song by Jeff Johnson as both the call to worship and the closing song. "Carried to the Table" by Leeland was used to continue the table theme. We created a backdrop CD of songs related to the word *table* found by searching iTunes. (My friend Josh Gaffga, a worship director from Denver, also wrote a great Taizé-like song for this Prayer Experience when we curated this worship experience for pastors there. For a copy of it, email him at gaffga@gmail.com.)

General Supplies:
- Tables of various sizes
- Various types of tablecloths (checkered, plain, etc., different colors that can be placed on top of canvas tarps to add color, depth, and decoration)
- Canvas tarps for bottom layers as needed and one to write on
- Table setting stuff: Bowls (wooden and crockery types), wooden spoons, crockery type cups and plates, chalice, baskets, etc.
- Candles and rope or white Christmas lights
- Bread of various kinds
- Signs printed out
- Elements for individual stations as listed

Prayer Station 0: Introduction to Tables Experience

(You can pick a spot to read the introduction to participants as they enter the worship space; or you can pass it to them on printed sheets to read individually; or you can create a sign for everyone to read simultaneously. See accompanying CD for text.)

Prayer Station 1
Psalm 23: God Prepares a Table

Scripture: Psalm 23

Purpose: God desires us to be reconciled, to be at peace with our friends and neighbors. We're called by Jesus to love our enemies and pray for those who persecute us. At this station, participants will consider the 23rd Psalm in a new light. They'll take the time to consider the people or groups with whom they are enemies...with whom they need to sit at the table, the people with whom they need to be reconciled.

Activity/Response: Participants will eat a candy as a symbol of their willingness to sit at this table and will take home an invitation as a reminder to live out this love and reconciliation with their enemies.

Supplies:
- Table with nice tablecloth or canvas with a colorful overcloth
- Candles and candleholders (like those used at a banquet)
- Plates or trays in silver/gold
- Candy (more than enough for entire group)
- Invitations printed (enough for entire group) to take home
- Signs
- Other lighting as desired (rope or white Christmas lights)

Setting Up the Station: Create a table that looks like a banquet table. Cover the table (round or long rectangular) with a nice tablecloth. Use nice china or "charger" plates in silver or gold (these can be found at Hobby Lobby for less than $2 each). Include nice candleholders and candles. Place the candy on a plate or tray in the center of the table and a tray or plate with invitations on it at one end. Place signs so they are easy to read and follow. The table can be highlighted with other lighting if desired.

Signs/Directions: On accompanying CD

Prayer Station 2: The Calling of Levi

Scripture: Luke 5:27-30

Purpose: Jesus sat around the table with all the wrong people. He often got in trouble with the Pharisees and other religious leaders because he chose to be with and bring life to the outcasts of society, such as Levi (Matthew), who became one of his trusted disciples. Jesus said he came for the sick, not the well, and he came to bring life—in abundance—for those poor in spirit and in need of healing.

Activity/Response: Participants will consider the calling of Levi and the other outcasts with whom Jesus regularly spent time. They'll write on a Band-Aid the names of people who need the love of Jesus in their lives; and then they'll choose to wear a Band-Aid to remind them to spend time with the outcasts and broken people in their lives and in the world.

Supplies:
- Tableware (crockery bowls, plates, wine glasses), bread, and grape juice; or party supplies if going with the party theme, such as gift bags or balloons.
- Band-Aids
- Black markers
- Signs
- Other lighting as desired (rope or white Christmas lights)

Setting Up the Station: Place a canvas tarp or other tablecloth on the table. You can use party bags or other decorations for a party or simply use items that might have been present at a dinner during Jesus' time (e.g., bread and goblets/cups, etc.). You could add coins to the station as a reminder that Matthew was a tax collector. Add candles or other lighting as needed. Hang or display signs so they're easily read.

Signs/Directions: On accompanying CD

Prayer Station 3
Table Interrupted: Jesus Anointed by a Sinful Woman

Scripture: Luke 7:36-50

Purpose: Participants will read about the dinner party at the Pharisee's home where a woman interrupts the party, displaying her extravagant love for Jesus by anointing him with expensive perfume. They'll reflect on the story and where they might be in it. They're invited to consider giving their best to Jesus.

Activity/Response: Participants will be invited to smell and even put on "perfume" as a symbol of giving their best, their all, to Jesus and accepting his great love for them.

Supplies:
- Table and covering
- Fancy jar or pitcher/container to hold "perfume"
- "Perfume" (we used a lavender or almond liquid soap rather than perfume due to allergies. Try "healing garden" brand, especially the organic kind, or lavender liquid soap)
- Signs
- Other lighting as desired (rope or white Christmas lights)
- Other decorations as desired

Setting Up the Station: The scene is a table at the home of a Pharisee. Set up the table with a canvas cloth and some colorful overcloth. Have a fancy jar or pitcher on the table filled with good-smelling perfume. The jar should be the focal point of the table. Set up signs so they're easily read. The rest of the table decoration can reflect a meal during Jesus' day, or you might even set it with a contemporary feel for a unique juxtaposition.

Signs/Directions: On accompanying CD

Prayer Station 4: At the Table with Mary and Martha

Scripture: Luke 10:38-42

Purpose: This station provides a mini-Sabbath at the table and along the journey.

Activity/Response: After reading the Scripture, participants will consider the story of Mary and Martha and where they (the participants) are in the story. They will have the time and space to just sit and have a conversation with Jesus.

Supplies:
- Table and tablecloth
- Mixing bowl and spoon
- Other items that suggest preparing a meal
- Dish towels
- Signs
- Candles
- Other lighting as needed
- Chairs and/or floor pillows/cushions

Setting Up the Station: Create a station with a kitchen table atmosphere. Set out a large mixing bowl (wooden bowl with a wooden spoon would be nice) and a couple of dish towels and some other dishes or bowls on the table, as if someone is preparing a meal. You could also add real grapes or bread for added decoration. Have two chairs at the station for sitting or have cushions on the floor where people can sit down and be with Jesus. Have signs displayed so they're easy to read and follow; light station as desired. A couple of large candles would be a great choice.

Signs/Directions: On accompanying CD

Prayer Station 5
Trouble at the Table: Washing the Cup

Scripture: Luke 10:38-42; 11:37-41 (see also *The Message* versions of these passages)

Purpose: This station acts as a confessional as students consider where they are with Jesus, and how they relate to God and to the poor of the world.

Activity/Response: Participants will turn out their pockets and read the Scripture passage. Participants will each wash a cup as they consider the condition of their own hearts. Is the outside different from the inside? Are they clean before God? Are they living out what they believe, and what Jesus desires for them?

Supplies:
- Dishpan or other large bin filled with soapy water
- Dishpan filled with clean water
- Dish drainer (optional)
- Sponges or dish brush
- Dish towels or paper towels
- Several coffee cups or mugs to be washed
- Signs
- Lighting as needed

Setting Up the Station: Create a table that can stand getting wet. Set up the station to look like a kitchen table. Use a checked tablecloth or other tablecloth found in a kitchen of today. Set up two wash/dishpans with water and soap and have several cups available for washing. Towels for drying hands should be close by. Hang or place signs so they're easy to read and won't get wet. Light station as needed.

Signs/Directions: On accompanying CD

Prayer Station 6
Table Excuses: Jesus at a Pharisee's House

Scripture: Luke 14:1-14; 15-24

Purpose: We all get busy and tired. We all get afraid and have doubts. Sometimes these things and other things get in the way of our participation and enjoyment of the great gifts, the banquet table that God provides for us. This station will give participants an opportunity for confession of the excuses we all make.

Activity/Response: Participants will read Luke 14 and consider where they choose to "sit" at life's banquet. Then they'll each write down on a paper plate the excuses they make for not coming to the banquet that Jesus provides and invites us to.

Supplies:
- Table with tablecloth
- Nice plates and glasses
- Paper plates
- Pens
- Signs
- Lighting, including candles and candlesticks even if you don't light them.

Setting Up the Station: Create a banquet table by covering a table with a tablecloth. Use nice china and glasses and/or nice candles and holders. Place paper plates around the table (could be placed on top of the china plates). Have pens available for writing on the paper plates. Have signs hung or placed on menu stands so they're easily read and followed. Use additional lighting as needed.

Signs/Directions: On accompanying CD

Prayer Station 7: Last Supper

Scripture: Luke 22:14-30; John 13:1-17

Purpose: To consider the table conversations at the Last Supper and provide an opportunity for students to write out their prayers while considering their own fears and questions

Activity/Response: They'll think about their own lives in the last year and write their prayers on the tablecloth, telling Jesus about their needs, thanksgivings, etc.

Supplies:
- Table with canvas dropcloth (or rolls of brown butcher paper—the kind for mailing packages)
- Sharpie markers in multiple colors
- Bread
- Grape juice in chalice
- Basket or plate for bread
- Signs
- White miniature lights
- Painting (or print) of Last Supper (optional). Could even have an artistic student design one for this experience.

Setting Up the Station: Cover table in a canvas tarp that can be written on with Sharpie markers. This tarp can be used again for a table or wailing (prayer) wall or for an "altar cloth" for future Communion or worship times. Or another option is to cover the table with brown butcher paper and have various colored Sharpie markers on the table or in a basket. (Make sure if using paper that the markers don't bleed through it.) Have a few prayers written out on the cloth/paper before worship starts so people get the idea. Have symbols of the Last Supper on the table: Bread and grape juice, chalice, etc., or you can use a print/painting of the Last Supper for a visual (not a cheesy one, please!). Hang signs behind table so there's plenty of room for writing prayers on the cloth. (Note: If you have a large crowd, check to see if the cloth needs moving during the course of the prayer time. Light with white miniature lights.)

Signs/Directions: On accompanying CD

Prayer Station 8: On the Road to Emmaus

Scripture: Luke 24:13-35

Purpose: To remind participants to take the time to look for Jesus, recognize Jesus in others along the way, and offer hospitality—because that's an important way we see Jesus and share him with others

Activity/Response: Participants will sample bread and try on sunglasses, helping them recognize Jesus along the way and in other people.

Supplies:
- Table and tablecloth
- Loaf or pita bread (enough for everyone to sample)
- Baskets for bread and sunglasses
- Grapes for decoration in a basket or bowl
- Wine chalice or crockery cups
- Pairs of sunglasses (various kinds, try the Dollar Store or collect old pairs)
- Candles and/or other lighting
- Signs

Setting Up the Station: Cover the table with a tablecloth. Decorate like a dinner table either in our day or in Jesus' day. Have a basket with bread and a wine chalice or crockery cups. Have a basket filled with sunglasses, and you can use grapes for added decoration. Display signs so they're easy to read and follow. Use a candle or two and other lighting as desired.

Signs/Directions: On accompanying CD

Prayer Station 9: Table by the Sea (Breakfast by the Beach)

Scripture: John 21:1-14; 15-19

Purpose: We all need to be reminded that God knows our futures and cares about the details of our lives here and now. This station reminds us that Jesus is providing for us before we are even aware of it. He has cooked breakfast for us before we even arrive. It also gives participants an opportunity to talk to Jesus about the questions and fears they have about their lives and futures.

Activity/Response: Participants will read John 21 and each consider their need for direction and provision. They will eat some goldfish crackers as a symbol and reminder that God is providing for them.

Supplies:
- Table with red-checked tablecloth
- Basket or two
- Goldfish crackers (enough for everyone to have several)
- Signs
- White miniature lights
- Fishnet and sea shells (found at craft stores)

Setting Up the Station: Set up a picnic table with a red-checked tablecloth, a basket filled with goldfish crackers, and a fishnet draped on the side. Use other baskets or a few sea shells for decorations. Display signs and Scripture so they're easy to read and follow. Light station with white twinkle lights.

Signs/Directions: On accompanying CD

Prayer Station 10: Art Table

Activity/Response: Create a station for an artistic response to the tables where Jesus sat and taught. Have art supplies available and tape so participants can share their prayers with others.

Prayer Room
DO JUSTICE

This Prayer Room was designed for the 2007 Bread for the World Conference in Washington, D.C. The Prayer Room was based on the theme of the conference—"Sowing Seeds: Growing a Movement"—and the theme verse from Micah 6:8:

> *He has shown all you people what is good.*
> *And what does the LORD require of you?*
> *To act justly and to love mercy*
> *and to walk humbly with your God.*

The stations also reflect several of the Millennium Development Goals to end global poverty and hunger. The purpose of this Prayer Room is to help participants pray for and become more aware of the need to live out justice and mercy in our daily lives.

General Supplies: Maps of the world and various continents, globes, photos of global events and people, groups and causes, anything that has an international flavor such as a tapestry, piece of pottery, hat, or art piece. Also you will need a large wooden cross.

Prayer Station 0: Intro Station

Setting Up the Station: This station is just a simple sign. It can be hung at the entrance to the prayer space or it can be printed and handed out as participants enter.

Signs/Directions: On accompanying CD

Prayer Station 1: Sowing Seeds

Scripture: 2 Corinthians 9:6-7; Psalm 65:9-13

Purpose: This station gives participants the opportunity to pray about sowing love, mercy, and justice in our world and taking the kingdom of God into the dark places and the regular places of our world.

Activity/Response: Participants will plant a seed as they consider where they're sowing the kingdom of God, and how they'll live out justice and mercy in their lives. They'll take home a seed to remind them to live justly and live out the kingdom of God.

Supplies:
- Large flower pot/window box or metal washbasin filled with potting soil
- Potting soil to fill flower box (use bag for decoration)
- Seed packets for decoration
- Sunflower seeds to plant and take home
- Garden gloves and trowel or two for decoration
- Signs and Scripture
- Table and covering
- Lighting as desired (we found a strand of white lights that had watering cans on them—just for fun but not necessary at all)

Setting Up the Station: Create a gardening area. Use elements of a gardener to create the vibe. Cover the table with a tablecloth and place the large basin of potting soil, garden gloves, seed packets, etc., as the focal point of the station. Have a basket or a small dish of sunflower seeds near the pot so they can be easily planted. Have enough sunflower seeds to plant and to have one to take home. Run a string of white lights through the station to highlight the items. Place or hang signs to that they're easily read and followed. (Note: We used the edible sunflowers as the seeds because they were inexpensive—and in case anyone tried to eat them, they'd be okay.)

Signs/Directions: On accompanying CD

Prayer Station 2: Praying Globally!

Scripture: Ezekiel 22:30 (NLT)

Purpose: Gives participants the opportunity to pray for the regions/continents of the world and the needs in these places.

Activity/Response: Participants will look at various maps and pray for the aid/relief workers, missionaries, governments, etc., in these places.

Supplies:

- Maps of the continents of the world (we found these at 1/2 Price Books; many were maps from old *National Geographic* magazines); we laminated the maps for protection and so they could be used again.

Setting Up the Station: Hang maps on a wall or tape them on the floor (if they are laminated) or display on a table. Hang or place signs around the table so they're easily read. Light station as needed.

Signs/Directions: On accompanying CD

Prayer Station 3: Water Station

Scripture: John 7:37-39; Psalm 65:1-13

Purpose: More than a billion people are without clean drinking water and sanitation. This station will help participants be thankful for the clean water they have and help them think of ways they can save water and help those who don't have clean water.

Activity/Response: Participants will drink a cup of water as they pray for people who don't have clean drinking water. They'll also pray about how they can save water themselves. (Optional response: Participants can donate money to water charities and/or take home a list of Web sites and organizations helping those who need clean water.)

Supplies:
- Water bottles of various kinds and brands
- Large water jug to supply water for all participants
- Water buckets
- Small paper cups
- Small can for trash
- Signs
- Handouts with water-aid-related Web sites and organizations (optional)
- Table and covering
- Lighting as needed

Setting Up the Station: Set up a table with a covering and place water jugs and cups for water on the table. Use the various water bottles and water buckets for decoration of the station. Hang or display signs and Scripture so they're easy to read and follow. If you're collecting money for a water charity, place bottles for collecting money on the table.

Signs/Directions: On accompanying CD

Prayer Station 4: Art Station

Activity/Response: Create a station for an artistic response to justice-related issues. Have art supplies available and tape so participants can share their prayers with others.

Signs/Directions: On accompanying CD

Prayer Station 5: Praying the News

Scripture: Micah 6:7-8; Philippians 4:5-7; 1 Thessalonians 5:16-17

Purpose: Participants will be challenged to see newspapers and news magazines (and news reports and news Web sites outside of the station) as opportunities for prayer rather than worry, fear, or frustration.

Activity/Response: Participants will read articles from newspapers and news magazines and pray for what they've read about.

Supplies:
- Copies of newspapers (local and national) and magazines
- Signs and Scripture
- Table and covering if needed
- Lighting as needed
- Chairs and/or floor cushions so participants can sit and read

Setting Up the Station: Hang or display newspapers on a table (or as we did, over a chalkboard). Display signs so they're easily read. Light station as needed. Have seating available so people can sit and read.

Signs/Directions: On accompanying CD

Prayer Station 6: Ending Slavery

Scripture: Isaiah 61:1-3; Amos 5:21-24 (especially verse 24)

Purpose: To make participants aware of the fact that slavery continues around the globe and that followers of Jesus need to take a stand against it and help work for freedom and justice for all people, especially children

Activity/Response: Participants will read stories and look at photos of children in slavery and forced child labor. They will pray for those in slavery, for the slaveholders, and for the people working to free these people around the globe. They will write their names on a chain link (made from construction paper) and add it to the chain as a symbol of solidarity and a desire to end global slavery and work for justice.

Supplies:
- Black construction paper cut in strips (enough for all participants)
- 2 or 3 staplers
- Basket to hold paper strips
- Paper chain of links made from black construction paper
- Package of oil pastels
- Photos of forced child labor (magazines or download from Internet)
- Signs and Scripture
- Stories of freedom/slavery
- Table and covering as needed
- Lighting as needed
- Print list of Web sites for participants to take home and look up after the experience (optional)

Setting Up the Station: Set up the station with the table and covering. Create a paper chain of links from strips of black construction paper. Chain can be hung or laid across the table itself. Cut more black construction paper into strips and place in a basket. Place a box of oil pastels near the basket to write on the chain links. Place or hang signs so they're easily read and followed. Put photos around the station to highlight the need for ending slavery worldwide.

Signs/Directions: On accompanying CD

Prayer Station 7: Healing Our World

Scripture: Matthew 5:3-5; 7-10

Purpose: To pray for healing for our world, for our friends, and ourselves. This is an opportunity to pray against the pain and violence in our world.

Activity/Response: Each participant will pray for healing for the violence and pain in our world and pray specifically for friends and themselves by writing names on a Band-Aid and placing it on the cross. Each participant will wear a Band-Aid as a reminder to continue to pray for healing in our world.

Supplies:
- Band-Aids (enough for at least two per person)
- Basket for holding Band-Aids
- Basket for trash
- Large wooden cross
- Sharpie markers
- Signs
- Table and covering as needed
- Lighting as needed

Setting Up the Station: Use a large wooden cross if available or create a cross from paper on a floor or wall. Cover a table and place a basket of Band-Aids on it with Sharpie markers nearby. Place an additional basket nearby for trash. Hang or place signs so they're easy to read. First write your own name on a Band-Aid and place the Band-Aid on the cross so participants will know what to do. Light station as desired.

Signs/Directions: On accompanying CD

Prayer Station 8: Praying for Your Country

Scripture: Ezekiel 22

Purpose: To provide an opportunity to pray for your country and its leaders

Action/Response: Participants will write their prayers for their country and its leaders on sticky notes and place them on a map of their country.

Supplies:
- Map of your country
- Sticky notes
- Sharpie markers
- Signs and Scripture
- Table and covering if needed
- Lighting as desired
- Place photos and articles about current events around the table

Setting Up the Station: Hang a map of your country on a wall or place it flat on a table. Have several stacks of colored sticky notes available along with markers or pens. Place signs so they are easily read and followed. Use lighting that works for the station.

Signs/Directions: On accompanying CD

Prayer Station 9: Jesus Holds All Things Together

Scripture: Colossians 1:18-20 (*The Message*)

Purpose: In a crazy and confusing world, life can sometimes feel out of control. This station reminds us that God is still in control and is holding together all the pieces of our lives and all the craziness of the world. This station will help students pray for the broken pieces in the world and in their own lives.

Activity/Response: Participants will consider the vast broken pieces of our world and the good as well as broken pieces of their own lives and give them to Jesus to hold. They'll hold a piece of a puzzle in their hands while praying, and then they'll take a piece home to remind them that God is holding all the pieces together.

Supplies:
- 1,000-piece jigsaw puzzle from which you can give away the pieces
- Basket to hold puzzle pieces
- Another puzzle box or two
- Table and covering
- Lighting as desired
- Signs and directions
- Photos of world problems/brokenness (optional)

Setting Up the Station: Cover table with tablecloth and place signs where they're easily read. Place a string of lights through the middle to highlight the signs. The focus of the station is the puzzle box and the plate or basket filled with puzzle pieces. If you use photos of world issues, display them around the basket of puzzle pieces. Place an extra sign or card in or near the puzzle pieces to remind people to take home a piece.

Signs/Directions: On accompanying CD

Prayer Station 10: Take a Stand…Live Justly

Scripture: Isaiah 58:6-12; Isaiah 43:19; Ezekiel 22:23-31; Micah

Purpose: This station helps bring home the ideas of this Prayer Experience. The participants will actually write down what they'll do and how they'll live out justice in their day-to-day lives, as well as how they'll take a stand for justice and mercy. They'll trace their feet on a piece of paper and then on a canvas tarp as tangible reminders of what they'll do to live out justice. They'll take home the paper tracing so they'll remember to live it out.

Activity/Response: Participants will trace their feet on a canvas tarp and on a piece of paper and write in both outlines what they'll do to show justice and love to their world.

Supplies:
- Canvas tarp that can be written on (or large sheet of butcher paper)
- Pieces of colored construction paper
- Colored Sharpie markers
- Signs
- Table and covering as needed
- Lighting

Setting Up the Station: Place a canvas tarp on the floor with a table beside it. Trace a couple of sample footprints on the tarp and write prayers in them so students will know what to do. (If necessary use a large piece of butcher paper instead of canvas—the idea of the canvas is that you can continue to use it and continue to add prayers to it for weeks to come). On the table place a basket of colored markers and construction paper. Allow room for writing down prayers. Place signs where they can easily be read and followed and highlight with rope lights or white mini-lights. Use an additional sign to remind students to take home their footprint papers. Make sure there's enough room for moving around and tracing feet.

Signs/Directions: On accompanying CD

Prayer Station 11: Reduce Child Mortality and Improve Maternal Health

Scripture: Matthew 19:12-13; Mark 9:36-37; Luke 18:15-16

Purpose: Jesus had special compassion for women and children—especially in honoring them when the culture of his day did not. In today's world of hunger, poverty, war, and natural disasters, women and children still suffer most. This station is based on two of the eight Millennium Development Goals: Reducing child mortality and improving maternal health. For more information go to Bread for the World (http://www.bread.org) and http://www.un.org/millenniumgoals.

Activity/Response: Participants will pray for the women and children of our world and consider their suffering. They'll put on some baby lotion to remind them to pray. The scent will be the reminder.

Supplies:
- Table with tablecloth
- Photos of women and children around the world (look for these in magazines, newspapers, and on the Internet)
- Baby lotion that actually has a scent—one or two bottles depending upon size of your group. (Hint: Baby lotion is also a great reminder of resurrection and new life and a bottle can be passed around a group during or following a talk/teaching on resurrection.)
- Signs
- Lighting as desired

Setting Up the Station: Cover a table with a cloth and arrange photos of women and children around the signs. Place the bottles of baby lotion within easy reach of participants. Add a sign to remind them to actually put on some lotion.

Signs/Directions: On accompanying CD

Prayer Station 12: Eradicate Extreme Poverty and Hunger

Scripture: Matthew 10:41-42 (NLT); 6:25-27; 14:15-21; 15:32-39; 25

Purpose: To help people gain a perspective on local and global hunger issues and how they relate to their own use of food. This is also based on a Millennium Development Goal to "eradicate extreme poverty and hunger." Please check out Web sites like Bread for the World and the ONE campaign for more information to use at this station (http://www.bread.org/learn/hunger-basics and http://www.one.org).

Activity/Response: Participants will consider the huge issue of hunger and pray about how they view and use food. Each will write their prayers on a paper plate and leave them on the table, giving them to Jesus.

Supplies:
- Table with covering
- Printed statistics relating to local and global hunger issues
- Paper plates
- Pens for writing out prayer on plates
- Food items such as rice and beans, as well as a pizza box or other food items to contrast the rice and beans
- Empty bowl
- Cross (optional)
- Lighting as needed
- Signs

Setting Up the Station: Cover the table with a tablecloth. The cloth could be a picnic cloth or fancy cloth for one half of the table and a piece of burlap for the other as a contrast of wealth and poverty. Place signs so they're easily read and followed. Have a stack of paper plates with pens available and space on the table to write out prayers. Have items of food on the table as decorations: Rice, beans, etc., as well as a pizza box or other food items to contrast the rice and beans. (Optional: A cross to place near the paper plates.) Place signs so they're easily read and followed. Create "sample plates" and place them on the table or near the cross. Light station as desired.

Signs/Directions: On accompanying CD

Prayer Station 13: Wailing Wall

Note: Wailing walls can be used with any Prayer Experience. Just place a verse or a certain focus for prayer on a sign and provide pens/markers for people to write out their prayers.

Scripture: Amos 5:24

Purpose: To allow students to respond to the issues of justice in written prayers

Activity/Response: Students will write out their prayers on the paper wailing wall.

Supplies:
- Large roll of butcher paper (or a whiteboard with whiteboard markers, or even a chalkboard with chalk)
- Multicolored markers, preferably the washable kind
- Signs
- Lighting as needed

Setting Up the Station: Use a large roll of butcher paper or bulletin board paper in a color that goes with your setup. Hang the paper on the wall; you can make it as large as you like, and you can double the layer of the paper as needed. We've also used whiteboards when they are already present in the room.

Signs/Directions: On accompanying CD

Prayer Experience
THE LIFE OF DAVID

Purpose: This Prayer Experience, based on 1 and 2 Samuel, is designed to help participants engage in the life of David. It stimulates a tangible response to Scripture and provides a holistic space to respond to the moving of the Holy Spirit, as well as a Chill Space for quiet reflection and journaling, Prayer Stations based on David's life, an opportunity to pray for our world, and an art space for creating two- and three-dimensional prayers.

General Supplies:

- Tablecloths or table coverings (keeping a similar color or texture going through all the Prayer Stations helps visually)
- Lighting: Candles, rope lighting, etc.
- Signs/directions printed out
- Scripture passages printed out
- Frames or stands for signs
- Blue painter's tape for hanging signs

Caution: Avoid too much red. The first time we created this experience, we had two large red hearts, one on the floor under the cross and another on the far wall of the Prayer Room. We also used red tablecloths. This caused some folks to think "Valentine's Day" rather than the heart of God. Also too much red is not relaxing to see or experience. The Valentine's Day concept would be great if you were doing this Prayer Experience/room during February. But I would recommend not using red tablecloths and toning down the red and perhaps eliminating the heart on the wall so the room doesn't visually scream Valentine's Day to some people.

Welcome/Introduction to Prayer Room/Prayer Experience:

As students enter the room, they're invited to remove their shoes and reminded that they're entering a holy space—a quiet place of worship and prayer, a contemplative space.

This message can be on a large poster sign and on a photocopied handout for folks to read as they enter the Prayer Room. Hang the sign in the entrance or place it on an easel for display where those entering can easily read it; have a stack of handouts on a table as they enter.

Intro Station: After entering or right at the entrance, create a station with a table that includes symbols of David's life arranged in an attractive manner. Such items might include a slingshot, five stones, a crown, a sword, a psalm written out or printed in calligraphy on a scroll-like piece of paper. This station could also be the spot for the handouts listed above.

Supplies:
- Table and covering
- Lighting
- Symbols of David's life: slingshot, five stones, a crown, a sword, a psalm written out or printed in calligraphy on a scroll-like piece of paper
- Signs/Directions

Signs/Directions: On accompanying CD

Prayer Station 1: Samuel the Prophet/Walking to Bethlehem

Scripture: 1 Samuel 16:1-13 (additional references: 1 Samuel 1:9-18; 3:1-11; 8:4-9; 10:1-2; 17-26, 13:6-14; 15:22-23)

Purpose: This station introduces the story of David. It begins with the prophet Samuel journeying to Bethlehem, where God sends him to anoint the new king of Israel.

Activity/Response: Participants will have some of the background for Samuel's trip to Bethlehem, and as they walk down the path, they'll consider how God is directing them and might be changing their assumptions. This station also has a place for washing hands as a symbol of giving up their fears and assumptions to God.

Supplies:
- Long tarp, folded if needed, to create a path 3 feet by 10 feet
- Brown wrapping paper (the kind used for wrapping packages)
- Sand
- Signs on frames to line the path
- Small table with covering
- Bowl of water and towel (additional pitcher of water as needed)
- Lighting for path and for table (rope lighting works great for highlighting the path)
- Copies or a large copy of 1 Samuel 16

Setting Up the Station: Create a pathway at least 10 feet long. This can be created with a long piece of cloth or a canvas tarp folded in thirds so it's three to four feet wide. Cover the canvas path with a piece of brown wrapping paper. You'll be making a paper path on top of the canvas path and thus save your canvas and allow for easier cleanup. The canvas base allows for less movement of the paper on the floor. Cover the paper with a thin layer of sand to make it look like a pathway. You may add some rocks along the sides for more realism if you'd like. Use rope lighting to highlight the edge or edges of the path. Place the signs on frames and have these line one or both sides of the pathway. Make sure the print is large enough to be read as one walks down the path. At the end of the pathway, set up a covered table, a bowl of water, and a towel.

Signs/Directions: On accompanying CD

Prayer Station 2: Praying for Our Families

Scripture: 1 Samuel 19; John 15:13

Purpose: David was the youngest of eight brothers. He was a shepherd, which wasn't the most respected job. David was also a great friend. He ended up as the best friend of King Saul's son, Jonathan. This station provides a space to consider David's role in his family and the participant's own family role. It also gives the participants opportunity to pray for their family members and to be a better friend.

Activity/Response: Participants will light a tea light or votive candle and place it in the sand as they pray for their family members and for their best friends.

Supplies:
- Various candles (recommend votives or tea lights)
- Lighter (long-handled torch type)
- Large vessel for sand, wading pool, bowls, trays filled with sand to act as candleholders/ bases for lit candles.
- Lighting: Candles, rope lighting, mini-lights, etc.
- Signs/directions and Scripture passages
- Table and covering

Setting Up the Station: Due to the number of participants in this Prayer Room, we used a child's plastic wading pool lined with a canvas tarp (to hide the color) and then filled it with sand. The canvas tarp is optional. We placed the pool on top of a round table so the action was waist high, but this could have also been placed on the floor. The candles were lit and placed in the pool filled with sand.

For a smaller number of participants, you can use trays (round glass, or metal, etc.) covered with sand as a base for the candles. Just make sure you have enough candles for all participants, a lighter, or another larger candle to light from—and be sure to monitor this station carefully due to open flames.

Signs/Directions: On accompanying CD

Prayer Station 3: Praying for Others

Scripture: 1 Samuel 16:6-10; 11-13; Matthew 7:1; Luke 6:37

Purpose: This station looks at the fact that David was the last to be included, to be invited to come to the party, when the prophet Samuel arrived to sacrifice and to anoint the next king of Israel. His father had left him in the fields taking care of the sheep. Too often we judge people by how they look or how old they are. Samuel was reminded by God not to judge anyone by outward appearances.

Activity/Response: Participants will consider whom they judge and whom they criticize, especially because of their outward appearance. They will pray for these folks and ask God's forgiveness for being judgmental and critical.

Supplies:
- Large sheet of red butcher paper cut in the shape of a large heart and taped to wall (or the outline of a large heart on wall or window/glass door.
- Sticky notes (heart-shaped if available) in bright neon colors (or participants could write names on the large heart without using sticky notes)
- Sharpie markers
- Table and tablecloth for place to write on
- Lighting: Candles, rope lighting, mini-lights, etc.
- Signs/directions and Scripture passages

Setting Up the Station: Cut out a large heart from red butcher paper (larger heart can be created by cutting two halves and taping them together) and hang it on the wall. Participants use neon-colored sticky notes to write down the names of folks they were praying for, and then they stick these notes on the large heart. A stained glass window effect can also be created by outlining a large heart on a window or large glass doors and allowing the notes to become the "colored glass" to fill in the heart. Another way to create a stained glass window effect is to use a drum screen (acrylic/Plexiglas screen used to muffle sound in front of the drum kit). Participants can put their sticky notes on both sides of the screen.

Signs/Directions: On accompanying CD

Prayer Station 4: Praying for Yourself and the Heart of God

Scripture: 1 Samuel 16:6-7; Psalm 139:13-16; John 17:20-23

Purpose: The Bible says that David was a man after God's own heart. It also says that God looks not at the outward appearance but instead at the heart...at our thoughts...intentions...motivations...passions, etc. Participants will consider what God's heart is like and how God feels about them. They will also take time to consider what's in their own hearts.

Activity/Response: Participants will write attributes/qualities of God's heart on paper hearts and also write down the feelings and emotions—the good things and the bad things—in their own hearts. After reading Scriptures that reflect God's heart for each of us, they will each write their names on a heart and pin them on a cross as a reminder of God's love and a symbol of giving their hearts to God. They will take home a small foam heart as a reminder of God's love for them and to seek God with all their hearts.

Supplies:
- Large wooden cross
- Two small tables
- Red butcher paper
- Clear contact paper
- Paper: Red photocopied with two hearts—heart of God and your heart
- Small foam hearts in a basket or dish to take home
- Thumb tacks to place hearts on the cross
- Lighting
- Signs and directions

Setting Up the Station: When we originally created this station, the large cross was the focal point of the room. We stood it in the center of the prayer space on top of a large paper heart we cut out of red butcher paper. Before standing the cross on the center of the heart, we covered the heart and floor area with clear contact paper so it would stick and not be torn as folks walked or stood on it. There were two small round tables on either side of the cross. One table held the signs and the stack of run-off hearts, pens, and an area to write about your own heart. In front of the cross was a basket with thumbtacks to hang hearts on the cross, and around the cross were the verses about God's heart. The second table held the basket of hearts to take home. We used the pre-cut foam hearts you can purchase at craft stores. We printed the hearts on an 8.5 x 11 sheet of red paper. We cut out the hearts to be hung on the cross and left the other side free. You could also write "heart of God" on the second heart or on this half sheet to distinguish the two. If you can find heart doilies at a party store on sale after Valentine's Day, these would also work for the hearts on the cross.

Signs/Directions: On accompanying CD

Prayer Station 5: Anointing Station

Scripture: Jeremiah 29:11-13; 1 Samuel 16:12-14

Purpose: This station provides an opportunity for participants to consider their calling and who God has designed them to be.

Activity/Response: They will make a cross on their foreheads with olive oil or anoint one another just as Samuel anointed David.

Supplies:
- Olive oil
- Paper towels
- Silver or silver-like tray for olive oil (royal look)
- Lighting: Candles in candleholders as on an altar
- Signs/directions and Scripture passages
- Table and covering

Setting Up the Station: Set up the station to look royal and sacred. Use a cloth or table covering that is easy to wash or one that can be thrown away due to the possibility of olive oil spills. Place a silver tray (or silver-gold/silver-like tray) on the table with a bowl or vessel with olive oil. Place a roll of paper towels or a cloth towel on the edge of the station for wiping hands. Use two candles in candleholders for this station. Place signs and Scripture so participants can easily read them.

Signs/Directions: On accompanying CD

Prayer Station 6
Killing Goliath: Looking at the Giants in Your Life

Scripture: 1 Samuel 17:12-57

Purpose: We all have things that yell at us and defy our faith in God just like Goliath defied the army of the living God. We all have broken pieces of our lives that God wants to heal. This station will allow participants to give these giants to God to defeat.

Activity/Response: Participants will take out five smooth stones just like David did getting ready to fight Goliath. They will consider and pray about the giants in their lives and take home a stone to remind them God has prepared them to fight and will help them defeat the giants in their lives.

Supplies:
- Vessel to hold water: Large backyard pond form or table-sized vessel
- Plants, large rocks, moss, etc., to make vessel look more like water found outside
- Smooth stones (gathered at a beach or lake or purchased at a craft store or dollar store); enough for all participants to have one.
- Signs and directions
- Rope lighting to outline the station
- Other lighting as desired

Setting Up the Station: We created a pool using a form for a backyard pond purchased at Lowes. We surrounded it with plants, rocks, and cloth so it looked like a real pond rather than just a form of a pool. This was created on the floor and participants sat on the floor to gather their stones from the pond. The pond had a layer of stones on the bottom and we had an extra supply of stones at the station. You can also set this up on a tabletop using a smaller-size vessel for the water. Surround the vessel with plants and rocks to remind participants that David was outside—not at a sink or bowl. Participants will have an opportunity to pray about the giants in their lives as they consider the giant Goliath.

Signs/Directions: On accompanying CD

Prayer Station 7: Whose Armor Are You Wearing?

Scripture: 1 Samuel 17:38-40

Purpose: Saul wasn't sure David was ready to fight Goliath. Saul wanted to prepare David his way. He offered David his own armor. But Saul's armor really didn't suit or fit David. David had been prepared by God to fight a different way. Too often we put on "armor" that others believe we need, or that we feel we need to protect ourselves. But that armor isn't from God and isn't helping us be who God created us to be.

Activity/Response: Participants will have the opportunity to pray about who God created them to be—children of the King.

Supplies:
- Armor (we found some plastic armor at a toy store)
- Shields (we borrowed some from a friend who collects them)
- Mirror
- Contemporary "armor": Football helmet, make-up, "label" clothing (brand named), shoes, etc.
- Cut-out masks printed (outline of a mask with eyes and mouth printed on white paper, cut out if you have time), enough copies for all participants
- Pens
- Table and covering
- Lighting
- Signs and directions
- Scripture

Setting Up the Station: Set up a Prayer Station on a 6-or 8-foot rectangular table with a tablecloth. Arrange symbols of contemporary armor on the table. These items might include sports gear, football helmet, soccer jersey, makeup samples, clothing and shoes that are status symbols. If you can borrow or make a shield and a helmet that looks like real armor, have these on or near the table display. Have a full-length mirror near the station or a mirror on the table itself. Provide a stack of photocopied paper masks and pens/pencils on the end of the table. Hang signs behind the table or on frames on the table. Make sure they're easy to follow. Light the station as you'd like, with either candles or rope lighting.

Signs and Directions: On accompanying CD

Prayer Station 8: David the Songwriter

Scripture: Psalm 15; 23; 27—or any of your favorites written by David

Purpose/Activity/Response: This station provides participants with an opportunity to think about all their favorite songs and the music that means something in their lives. It will also give them an opportunity to read some of David's songs and write their own praises in song, poem, or prayer form.

Supplies:
- Bibles open to the Psalms
- Favorite psalms, photocopied
- Paper, markers, pens (we used inexpensive spiral notebooks)
- Personal CD players (3 to 5 depending upon number of participants)
- Backdrop instrumental music or sounds of ocean
- Batteries (extras for CD players)
- Large floor cushions
- Low tables for writing
- Use a laptop and/or a projector to show slides of scenes from nature (optional)
- Or have photos of nature on a table or hung on a wall to look at as participants read the psalms and listen to the music.

Setting Up the Station: We set up a low table with a soft tablecloth and floor pillows. Participants sat on floor cushions to listen to the CDs and read the psalms and write their own praises as they watched a slide show of nature photos. You can create the same station at a table of regular height and use photos instead of a slide show. Have Bibles open to the Psalms and have specific psalms printed and photocopied to be read. Have paper, spiral notebooks, and pens on the table—and CD players, too.

Signs and Directions: On accompanying CD

Prayer Station 9: Honoring Your Enemies and Praying for Those Who Persecute You (and Praying for Our World)

Scripture: 1 Samuel 19:9-10; 11-14; 1 Samuel 24:1-22

Purpose: Saul became jealous of David, his victories, and his popularity. He spent lots of time and energy chasing David and trying to kill him in various ways. When David had the opportunity to kill Saul, he didn't take it because Saul was God's anointed king.

Activity/Response: This station gives participants an opportunity to pray for their enemies and enemies in the world.

Supplies:
- Map of your city/state, the United States, and the world
- Neon sticky notes
- Sharpie markers
- Photos of enemies cut from magazines and newspapers
- Signs and directions
- Table for writing

Setting Up the Station: This station works well on a wall. Hang the various maps on a wall. Tape signs and other photos of enemies and hateful situations around the world near or around the maps. Provide a table or other area with a basket for pens and neon sticky notes.

Signs and Directions: On accompanying CD

Prayer Station 10: Bathsheba (Opportunity to Repent)

Scripture: 2 Samuel 12:1-14; Psalm 51

Purpose: This is a station of confession. David's most famous sin was his adultery with Bathsheba. While he sinned "strongly," he also repented strongly.

Activity/Response: This station gives participants an opportunity to confess their sins and shred them in a paper shredder. An additional option is to provide a bowl of water for washing hands after shredding the sins. This can be omitted if you feel it's too repetitive after the ritual washing in Prayer Station 1.

Supplies:
- Table with space for writing
- Paper and pens
- Paper shredder
- Bowl of water to wash hands in and towels (paper or cloth) for drying (optional)
- Signs/directions
- Scripture passages (especially additional copies of Psalm 51)

Setting Up the Station: Provide a table or other area that has enough room for writing. Cover table with a covering that can get dirty or wet, depending upon whether you do the water option. A 6- or 8-foot rectangular table would work well for this station. Set out pieces of paper and pens or pencils, then the paper shredder. Make sure this station is near an outlet so you can plug in the paper shredder. Place the bowl of water and the towels at the end of the table. Have more than one copy of Psalm 51 available for reading—you might have additional copies so participants can take them home. Make sure signs are hung or placed so they're easily read and connect with the various activities.

Signs/Directions: On accompanying CD

Prayer Station 11: David as the Delivery Boy

Scripture: 1 Samuel 17:12-18 (especially vv. 17-18)

Activity/Response: At this station, participants will taste cheese crackers to remind them that God uses every experience in our lives for his glory. They will consider David's willingness to obey his father Jesse and take cheese and bread to his brothers in Saul's army. Thus, this Old Testament "pizza delivery guy" was in the right place at the right time to see Goliath. God used an everyday, mundane event to place David in just the right spot to fulfill God's great plan for him.

Supplies:
- Cheese crackers (enough for all participants to have some)
- Basket for crackers
- Table and covering
- Lighting
- Signs and directions

Setting Up the Station: Create a station with a covered table. Place a box of cheese crackers in a basket on the table with the signs placed or hung behind the table so they're easily read by participants. Have extra crackers available as needed. Use candles or rope lighting or other lighting as desired.

Signs/Directions: On accompanying CD

Additional Stations

Chill Space: The purpose of this space is to provide a quiet place for individual prayer, journal writing, Bible reading, and listening to God. This space will include an oasis-type center with sand, water (fountain(s) and bowls), and plants. It should be set up for relaxation and comfort with floor cushions around the core area. This can be its own Prayer Room within the Prayer Experience. We had a prayer room like this as part of our youth space/youth room—and it was open all the time.

Scripture: Psalm 46:10; Luke 5:16

Supplies:
- Sand
- Plants
- Fountains (we borrowed a couple of fountains from friends)
- Large floor pillows
- Large containers for water
- Bibles
- Journals/spiral notebooks/paper and pens
- Candles or other mood lighting

Setting Up the Space: Turn a corner of the room (or an alcove if you have one) into a quiet place to pray. Create an oasis in the center of this space using a plastic tarp covered with a canvas tarp, then a layer of sand. Shape this base into something other than a square or a circle. Place one or two basins of water in the center of the sand space. We raised one on a brick and used plastic terra-cotta-looking planters for the basins. Place plants around the basins and rocks to make it look natural. We borrowed plants, real and silk, from folks in our church. Place floor pillows, along with Bibles and journals and pens, around the oasis. Place candles around the oasis. Use only candles with glass covers or in glass containers. Other lighting sources, such as rope lights or white mini-lights, can be used as desired.

Wailing Wall: Like the Wailing Wall in Jerusalem, this space provides an opportunity for participants to write their prayers on a wall of paper. This can be placed in an area near the Chill Space or in some other part of the Prayer Room. Participants can also be directed to write poems, prayers, thoughts, and words from God (Scripture references) on the Wailing Wall.

Supplies:
- Two to four rolls of 50-foot, brightly colored butcher paper or brown wrapping paper
- Waterproof markers
- Tape that will hold for a day or a week depending on how long your Prayer Room lasts (Hint: Blue painter's tape or packing tape works best). Ask about what's okay to use on the walls of your space and test the tape and paper in advance of the Prayer Room to see what will allow paper to remain on the wall.

Signs/Directions: On accompanying CD

Art Space/Art Station

The Art Station provides a place to create prayers using various mediums, or art supplies. Participants create 2-D and 3-D prayers responding to what God has done or spoken to them about in the Prayer Room. Art mediums to be included are: Chalk and oil pastels, crayons, markers, clay, and old magazines that can be cut up and pasted for collages.

Supplies:

- Markers
- Crayons
- Paper of various sizes and colors (multicolored construction paper, drawing paper, black construction paper for oil pastels)
- Sketch books with nicer drawing paper
- Oil pastels
- Chalk pastels
- Colored pencils
- Clay (modeling clay that doesn't dry out is the easiest to use)
- Paper towels
- Scissors
- Glue sticks
- Containers for water if paints are used (not recommended if group is mostly middle schoolers!)
- Blue painter's tape
- Large roll of plastic and tape to cover carpet if paint is used
- Tables with plastic tablecloths to use as easels and creation spaces
- Signs/directions

Setting Up the Station: According to the size of the group participating in this Prayer Experience, set up one or two 8-foot tables with throwaway tablecloths (black works best). Put tables against the wall so you can hang signs and participants can hang up their artwork. Lay out the art supplies on the table with room to work in the front. Place two or three chairs at each table. Have someone draw or sketch a couple of prayer pieces to hang up as examples so participants will get the idea they can hang up their works, too. (Hint: Have someone monitor this station so it doesn't get too messy. This person can hang up artwork and put supplies back in an organized way.)

Signs/Directions: On accompanying CD